D0921772

LESSONS I LEARNED FROM

The Dogs Who Saved Me

The experiences related in this book are true according to my best recollections; no account has been embellished or fictionalized in any way.

For Sandy, Sapo, Alex, Niki, Ellie, Ian, Osa, Mystic and Harper. You have taught me more than these few words could ever express. I miss you every day, and you are in my heart forever.

Dedicated to the memory of all our beloved heroes:

Jed Dog * Luke * Jonah * Obadiah * Manfred * Kai * Bart * Dana * Goldie * Bella * Scooter * Lobo * Wolfen * Tramp * Courage * Beau * Rex * Bowser * Kelly * Petey * Sheba * Muffin * Barney * Harley * Pepper * Omi Kueckels * Duchess * Charmer * Xena * Trigger * Wilbur Downs Jacobson * Mikey Pavia * Alice Jacobson * Sugar Pavia * Seiko * Icis * Oscar * Saddie Girl * Sweet Lilly * Billie * Princess Belle Belle * Sunny Bear * Tonya * Sabby * Killer * Queenie's Prince Ebony * Suzy Snoopy Bennett * Sogi * Fina * Sopie * Rica * Sadie Trepp * Mustang Sally * Scooter Justus * Tippy * Honey * Rambo * Shy-Ann * Tanner Murray

Preface

As a personal preference, I generally do not read the preface to a book; any defense or qualifying remarks on the part of the author just serve to distract or prejudice me before I begin, and so I simply like to jump right in and begin reading the story. Given that inclination, I find myself now amused that I am attempting to write a preface to my own book, hoping that you will pause for a moment and consider my brief introduction before you flip the page.

First and foremost, thank you for purchasing this book, whether in hard copy or electronic format. I assure you that, just as the cover indicates, one hundred percent of my net profit from the sale of this book will go to animal rescue. In fact, the opportunity to make continuous donations to some very worthy rescue groups is one of the two reasons I wrote this book.

The other reason is to honor the canine heroes of my life.

While this book is categorized as a memoir in that it is a personal account of some of my own experiences, it is structured around the lives of six of my truest friends: Rufus, Sapo, Alex (& Niki), Ellie, Ian and Osa—with the tales of a few others included as well. A literary agent once told me that no one would want to read a memoir written by me because after all, she asked bluntly, "Who are *you*?" Nobody, I would answer. I'm nobody (which always puts me in mind of the Emily Dickenson poem of that title, a line of which reads, "How dreary to be somebody..."). My intention with this book is not to promote myself or give credence to anything I do or think or believe. Rather, as you will certainly realize, it is to compare the heroic nature of good dogs to the decidedly more flawed character of humans, myself especially.

If you love dogs as I do, I hope you will find your heart touched by the unconditional love and devotion of the dogs who saved me, and I hope your life, like mine, is enriched by the lessons they taught me. If that is the case, I further hope that you will honor them—and all good dogs—by making a donation to your local animal shelter or rescue group. Thank you in advance for doing so.

Prologue

The first meaningful dog in my life was a small Cocker Spaniel-Terrier mix named Sandy. She was the family dog, and our experiences with her taught me not only positive dog-parenting behaviors but also those behaviors I would never choose to follow with my own dogs later in life.

I remember the day Mom and Dad brought her home. The air was clear and warm—the kind of sunny California day that persuades folks from colder states to move here. We lived in a modest, three-bedroom home in Lakewood, a suburb of Los Angeles. I was six and in the first grade, just learning to read, and I loved the Dick and Jane series of early readers. In Dick and Jane's family, everyone was always kind to each other, and Mother and Daddy would often bring the children surprises. Once, they brought home a puppy. Reading these books created a practice which remains with me today—the inclination to escape a harsh world by losing myself in another more pleasant, though fictional, world.

Needless to say, my family was nothing like the one in Dick and Jane's world. Yet on this beautiful sun-drenched day, here were my Mom and Dad with a surprise for us, a wriggling, sweet-faced puppy. Someone had abandoned her outside the tavern where my maternal grandmother worked in L.A. Grandma called Mom and Dad, and they agreed to bring her home.

How could a little girl not fall in love with a puppy as it bounded through the grass toward her, ears flopping? Showered with a thousand puppy kisses, I had my first lesson in the unconditional love a good dog offers willingly every day.

She was our first family dog, and everyone indulged in doting on her, from feeding her treats to teaching her silly tricks. She became housebroken overnight, it seemed, and would go to the door to let us know when she wanted out. The silly tricks began with the standards: Speak. Shake hands. Sit up. Then my mother amazed us all (where had she learned the art of dog training?) by holding Sandy's muzzle in her hand and balancing one of the dog's favorite treats on her nose. When she moved her hand, Sandy would jerk her nose aside and catch the treat in her mouth before it hit the ground. Why will a dog willingly subject herself to this kind of behavior on the part of her humans? Certainly she must have thought us odd. Thank the powers of the Universe for the infinite patience in dogs. She not only put up with our shenanigans, she reveled in them, eager to please us, and we rewarded her for her unfailing cooperation by giving her far too many treats and by being gushingly and obnoxiously proud of her and her abilities.

I'm grateful to my parents for teaching me, at such a young age, that dogs are family members. They go where the family goes—for rides in the car or walks to the park—and they sleep where the family sleeps, indoors on someone's bed or in their own bed but close to one of their humans. Their care equals that of a family member as well. When Sandy was hit by a car after dashing into the street to chase a cat, my parents paid what must have amounted to an enormous vet bill to have her broken leg and other injuries mended. They never complained about the cost, and we learned to be more vigilant with her, to be careful of her safety at all times.

But in attempting to be the best pet owners they could be, my parents failed dismally in one particular aspect. In the early 1960's, it had become fashionable to enroll dogs in "obedience training." Because Sandy had not yet learned to walk well on a leash, and because my dad had for some reason taken a proprietary interest in her, it was decided that he would be the one to train her.

My father, at this time, was dying, though the disease which was undermining his health was as yet undiscovered. An extremely rare form of cirrhosis had begun to compromise his liver, subversively gathering his own natural enzymes into a mutinous mob amassed to bring him down, arbitrarily choosing my proud Irish-American father. He would live another several years, but already his strength was ebbing, and he felt unwell much of the time.

Dad set about to train Sandy as if he were taking in hand one of his children. This was before the enlightened days of affection training (either for animals or small children). Classes were scheduled, and we learned for the first time about the remarkable technology of the choke chain collar. This collar is to be worn only when the dog is being trained or walked. The chain fits loosely around the dog's neck but can be tightened quickly to 'choke' the dog if it is not in a frame of mind to comply or simply doesn't know what to do. A command is given, the dog responds—or else. People still use choke chain collars today. And I am just as amazed and abhorred at this prospect now as I was fifty years ago when I first learned of it.

Sandy had learned early on to seek sanctuary, when necessary, beneath my parents' bed. Their room was not carpeted, and their bed was the largest in the house, so the area beneath it provided almost a cave-like atmosphere. It was here that our little dog would retreat when she felt threatened or tired or just wanted to be left alone, especially on a hot summer's day. She would curl up on the hardwood floor back there in the darkness and sleep or cower, depending on the circumstances.

It was to this private place that Sandy would flee when she heard the jingle of the choke chain in my father's hand, causing him to begin their horrific practice sessions together on a bad note by dragging her out from under the bed and carrying her outside. By the time he'd gotten her to the sidewalk in front of the house and slipped the collar over her head, she would already be wild-eyed and frantic.

Fixing her in a sitting position on the sidewalk, he would set off walking with the command, "Heel, Sandy!" The problem was, she wouldn't walk with him. Her response to his harsh tone and rough treatment was instinctive; she would immediately adopt the submissive position, rolling onto her back, belly up. Dad interpreted this as disobedience. She did not *want* to heel, he assumed. In his tenacity, his resolute inflexibility, he determined to make her obey, to teach her that she *would* heel, whether she wanted to or not.

The first time I saw him drag her down the concrete on her back, writhing, choking, twisting, foaming at the mouth, snarling and snapping at the leash, was the last time I saw it. I retreated to the house, to the bedroom I shared with my sister, and wished for a sheltered, dark place to hide myself. Certainly it must be easier for a dog to endure the cruelty of a stranger than it is to endure this kind of betrayal at the hands of a beloved human. I could not imagine what our little dog was feeling. I couldn't bear to think of it. I wanted to comfort her, to somehow communicate to her that she did, indeed, have to do what my father commanded. No less than absolute immediate obedience would be tolerated. My father was a tough guy, a cop and a war veteran. He gave no ground to insubordination, especially not from small, helpless animals.

But I was just a little girl suffering a small loss of innocence and as such I was powerless to help her. So

I waited, biding my time behind the scenes as I often did, silently watching. Eventually my dad came back in the house, removed Sandy's collar, and laughed along with the rest of the family as she fled to her formerly safe haven in the bedroom. When everyone else became absorbed with other things, I crept quietly into my parents' room, got down on my belly on the floor and reached underneath the bed to pet and soothe the little trembling dog that lay panting there. She growled at me. I pulled my hand back, folded my arms and set my chin on them. I didn't speak because I didn't want to risk discovery. I remained there with her. It was the only comfort I could offer.

Over time and with a few more equally traumatic sessions, Sandy learned to "heel" on the leash, to stop when my father stopped, to duck around behind him and sit submissively by his side, awaiting further orders. Both human and dog, I'm sure, were relieved when this communication gap was finally bridged. After all, she really did want to please him, she just hadn't understood what it was he wanted. And he really did feel an affinity for the dog and a certain pride of ownership, which was no doubt partly to blame for the stubbornness in his rigorous training sessions with her; he couldn't have the neighbors see a little dog get the best of him.

I'll never know whether I am right or wrong, but I want to believe that my father—because he was not just Catholic, but Irish-Catholic—suffered at least some small amount of guilt over his treatment of Sandy in the obedience lessons, especially when she began to understand and to respond so well. Say what you will about people being created in the image of God; the truth about dogs and people is this: The four-legged ones are possessed of far more goodness than the two-legged ones and in that respect, dogs have a much greater capacity to forgive. Whether God or I ever forgave him is another matter. The truth is, the little dog did, and Sandy became his constant companion during the months that he wasted away at home, too sick to work and not sick enough—yet—to remain hospitalized. My mother had found a recliner chair for him so that he would be a bit more comfortable. He would lay himself back and Sandy would accomplish a jump of heroic proportion to lie beside him in the chair, both stretched out, the dog comfortable, the man struggling against the daily worsening pain.

For my father, I think, Sandy had served as a distraction. He had first her training, and then simply her companionship to focus on. Had she not been with him all those hours when we were at school and Mom was at work, he would have been profoundly alone.

The same would have been true for me, after my father's death, had it not been for Sandy. Once Dad left for the hospital the final time, I became a "latch key" kid, although the term was a misnomer in our era; we lived in a safe suburb at a time when, with most of the women home in the neighborhood during the day, we thought nothing of leaving our side door unlocked. Arriving home from school before my siblings, I would always be greeted at the door by a wagging tail and happy dog grin, and Sandy would follow me through the house, making herself finally comfortable beside me as I watched cartoons and waited for the house to fill with noise. There were days, too, when I stayed home from school sick, and she would lie alongside me in the bed, the only reassuring warmth in a cold, empty house. By the age of nine, I was already finding my loneliness a heavy burden to carry. Had she not been there, the silence I would have returned home to every day might have crushed me.

But somehow I will always remember Sandy in the context of my father. She lived for another decade after he died, but my memories of her after he was gone are vague. It was a big job for such a small dog, to carry some of the burden for my father along this last, horrendously difficult road of his life. Her task completed, she settled into an almost anonymous role in our family, present at all celebrations and important functions, but always and only in the background.

Rufus

CHAPTER ONE

Human beings are resilient, and it has been my experience that we can find our way through some very dark times, as long as we have hope that somehow there is light just beyond the shadow of darkness. But the absence of hope will ultimately lead to despair, and from there it is a short journey to the point at which we are ready to give up.

I have been to this point several times in my life, but by far the most critical time for me was at the age of fifteen. My young spirit was so brutalized in that year, I almost didn't survive. I am grateful now to the powers of the Universe for tossing me a life preserver in the form of a block-headed mixed-breed dog named Rufus.

The years leading up to that one weren't easy. Dad died just before I turned nine, leaving Mom to provide for and raise four young children on her own. A year later, however, my sister, Peggy, won a Shetland pony in a contest, so we had the thrill of this acquisition to the family. But it meant that Mom had one more mouth to feed. Knowing how much it meant to my sister (who was certifiably horse crazy) and believing that having them to care for would keep us out of trouble, Mom not only purchased an additional horse or two, she sold our home in Lakewood and bought horse property in nearby Orange County, so that we could have our horses in our own backyard, a dream come true for Peg.

Change is never easy. When we moved, I left behind several close friends whom I would have joined the following year in a special program for gifted kids—something that wasn't offered at my new school. But we were trying to recover from the trauma of losing a husband and father. Becoming involved with the horses gave us the opportunity for a change in life-style, a fresh start.

Peg's constant activity with the horses is what led her to meet our next-door neighbor, Art. He caught her one night sneaking into his barn.

On a sweltering summer night, we had listened to one of his horses kicking the door of its box stall for hours, until my sister couldn't take it any more. She climbed the fence, crept into the barn, and found the mare's water tub bone dry. She grabbed a hose and turned on the faucet, the horse greedily sucking up the water almost as fast as it poured into the tub.

It was about that time that Art showed up. My sister, a brash and defiant twelve-year-old, told him exactly what she thought of him leaving the horse without water. He laughed at her. Art had a way of chuckling in derision when he thought someone was being "ridiculous," which was pretty much anyone who didn't see the world through his eyes. Still, the two somehow became friends. He offered to let Peg ride his horses, and she, on many more occasions, hopped the fence to feed or water Art's horses when they'd been neglected.

My mother soon made Art's acquaintance as well, and despite the fact that Mom was ten years his senior and Art had a wife at home, the two began meeting at a local bar in the afternoons after work.

It is true of human nature, I suppose, that we often choose our partners not by virtue of pragmatic criteria, but rather by the way they make us feel. As a widow, my mother shrugged off the attentions of two very nice men who got on well with her children, and she chose instead the man who made her feel young and attractive.

Throughout my years of junior high, my mother and Art continued an on again, off again relationship that kept Mom away from home most evenings and left my siblings and me to fend for ourselves in terms of foraging for dinner. When I look back on it now, having raised my own four kids as a single mother, I see how much of an absentee parent Mom was. However, though the words went unspoken, we all felt Mom deserved her own happiness—as long as her happiness didn't disrupt our personal lives. Of course, it was only a matter of time....

Eventually, Mom pressed Art to declare himself; she wanted a husband and, as far as she was concerned, it could be him or someone else. My mother was strong-willed and beautiful. Few men said no to her.

Shortly thereafter, Art bought two acres of horse property in the "Inland Empire," in an unincorporated area west of Riverside known as Mira Loma. There was a ramshackle old house on the property, so Art pulled his Airstream trailer onto it, brought his horses up, and separated from his wife, who by now was dying of cancer.

All things considered, at the age of fourteen, I thought life was pretty good. I had made some good friends in Orange County. I had a boyfriend, Harold, who had a driver's license and a car. Mom wasn't home much, so I spent a lot of time riding our horses or just hanging out on the front porch, listening to rock 'n' roll and talking to my friends, occasionally running a brush through my waist-length brown hair.

But that was 1968. And the turbulent events not only in the world but in my personal life were about to sweep me down into the vortex of a prolonged clinical depression.

I had a great history teacher that year, Herbert Jehle, and due to his exuberant teaching and likeable personality, I became interested in politics. I had seen the ugliness of racism during the Watts riots of 1965, when we were still living less than ten miles from Los Angeles. Three years later, as I began to follow news events more closely, I appreciated Martin Luther King, Jr. as one of the most courageous heroes of his time. Then suddenly he was shot down in cold blood and my mind reeled. How could this be?

Robert Kennedy was running for President at the time, and in my history class I learned of his contribution to the Civil Rights Act and his opposition to apartheid in South Africa. The more I read about him, the more he became a hero to me, as King had been.

On June 4, 1968, I stayed up to watch the late news, to hear "Bobby" give his victory speech after winning the California primary. As he stepped down from the stage, I turned the TV off and went to bed, elated by his victory. Early the next morning, I awoke to news that he'd been shot moments after delivering that speech and had died in the night.

I was devastated. At fourteen, I was so young, so tenderhearted, so impressionable, that the two assassinations so close together filled me with anger and bitterness.

In the days following Kennedy's death, I felt hollow and sick inside. I had no energy, and I didn't want to go to school. I stayed home for a couple of days; it was the end of the year, and my teachers all seemed to have reached their end point. I found myself overwhelmed with a heavy, lethargic sleepiness. I would sleep for hours, but feel no better when I woke up. I tried to return to school, but was overwhelmed with nausea by the end of the day. Finally, Mom took me to the doctor.

I had mononucleosis.

One of my brother's friends, Kirk, had been infected with it some weeks earlier. When the boys came through the house after school each day, my brother and his friends were in the habit of opening our refrigerator and getting a big drink of milk, straight from the carton. It seems Kirk had left a few of his little bugs on the container—enough to make me severely ill.

I can recall very little of the days after my diagnosis. Summer began, and my friends—including my boyfriend—starting heading to the beach every day. I remained in bed all day every day, sicker than I'd ever been in my life. I was bored, lonely, and feeling abandoned by everyone. My birthday rolled around in July, and I turned fifteen, but I have no memory of it.

Finally, in August, I was strong enough to sit on the porch and talk to my friends for a few hours every evening. I was unattractively thin, my mouth was filled with painful sores from the mono, I hadn't kissed my boyfriend in months, but I was beginning to have hope that I might recover from all this by the time school started in September.

It was during that time that Mom announced that she'd be taking me and my sister up to Art's property in Mira Loma "for the weekend." I thought it odd that she intended to trailer our horses up. Fifty miles on a busy freeway is a long stretch to pull a trailer, especially considering that I still wasn't up to riding. But I never questioned Mom's intentions.

We arrived at "the ranch" (as it had been described to us) on a Friday evening. Temperatures had been in the eighties in Orange County, but farther inland away from the beach it was close to one hundred degrees. Peg and I were surprised by the heat but not discouraged. We'd actually been looking forward to the adventure. From Mom's description, "the ranch" offered a rural setting with miles of open space for rid-ing—just what two city girls with horses long for.

I suppose we had expected something like the Pon-derosa. What we found was anything but. Art's prop-erty sat on a long narrow street of rundown houses—nothing like our small but neat home in Orange County. His house was more empty shell than home. In the yard we saw a small metal travel trailer, which was where Art stayed.

We were still trying to take it all in as Mom drove through an open chain link gate and up a bumpy gravel driveway. Before we could get out of the car, we were greeted by two dogs. One was a small black and white terrier. The other dog was mostly white with a couple of large brown spots, one across half his face and one on his body. He was nearly the same size as the terrier, but he was clearly a puppy, with huge feet he had yet to grow into. He jumped on us with dirty paws, wagging his tail excitedly. Art strolled out to meet us, beer can in hand.

"That's Five," he said, pointing to the terrier and belching. "They left her here when they moved out. That's her pup. I gave all the rest of them away, but that one's so ugly, no one wants him. I call him Rufus." He kicked at the dog with his boot to make him get down, then laughed.

After we'd unloaded and settled the horses into Art's "pasture" (which turned out to be simply a large dirt field filled with tumbleweeds), Peg and I learned that our accommodations consisted of two small army cots set up under a pepper tree outside Art's trailer.

To our complaint, Art replied, "Well, you can sleep on the ground if you'd ruther," and once again he gave his derisive laugh.

We'd brought our brothers' sleeping bags, the same ones they'd used on camping trips years ago with our dad. The bags hadn't been out of the garage in a decade, and they smelled like it.

That first night, I was miserable.

By the time we went to bed, the air had cooled to a balmy eighty degrees. My sleeping bag was too hot and too smelly for comfort, so I ended up lying on top of it. I only had to lie still for a moment before the mosquitoes began to buzz around me. I could hear my sister cursing and slapping at her arms. And then there was that dog.

Rufus was a puppy, and I know that he just wanted to cuddle up with us, as puppies do, but he only succeeded in driving us crazy for hours, trying to climb onto our cots, trying to lick our faces. For every hundred times we pushed him down, he came back a hundred and one. I could see his need for love and affection, but at that point I wasn't feeling love for anyone, especially not a dirty, ill-mannered pup who was annoying the heck out of me.

Though I'd been recovering, I was still very weak and needed to sleep ten to twelve hours over the course of a day. I didn't get much sleep that night—or the next night either, as the same jumping dog circus act began the minute I tried to sleep. I hadn't been able to sleep during the day, as there was no place to take a nap where I wouldn't experience the same onslaught. My days consisted of sitting in a chair in the shade, repeatedly saying "No, Rufus, get down," as he tried to climb into my lap, but trying not to move around much in the intense heat. Nights were spent trying to get at least a few hours of sleep. I couldn't wait to go home.

Nearly a week later, we were still in Mira Loma. I'd been asking Mom for days when we'd be going home. Her responses were terse and dismissive.

"Why can't you just relax and enjoy your time up here?" she would snap in irritation, then turn away.

The thing is, there was nothing really for me to "enjoy." I had no friends there. My pony was there, but I still couldn't do much other than make lethargic trips out to the field to feed her carrots and brush her. There was nothing of a recreational nature in the area—no parks or playgrounds. Peg and I played cards and talked about horses—and boys, which only made me miss my boyfriend all the more.

Then on Saturday, out of the blue, my oldest brother showed up at the ranch. He drove up in Mom's Impala, which we'd left at home, since we'd ridden up in Art's truck, pulling the horse trailer. Dan was twenty-two and hadn't lived at home for years, but he and Mom were close.

"Your brother's here to take you home," she told us. I was just as confused as I was elated. I didn't understand what was going on. Mom had become detached and secretive in the years since she'd begun dating Art, and this moment was no different. She wouldn't offer any explanations. Dan would drive us back home to Orange County, but we had to leave without our horses.

This was like telling us that we could finally go home, back to our friends and our own beds and all that was familiar—but we had to leave our legs behind. Our horses were an extension of our personalities. We rode every day (at least I did when I was healthy) and constantly worked on schooling our horses and practicing horsemanship in order to be successful in the horseshows we entered on a regular basis. It is not an understatement to say that our lives revolved around our time spent with them.

And now Mom was telling us we had to leave them behind. We'd been grounded before, restricted from riding for inappropriate behavior. But this was something different. We hadn't done anything wrong other than to be unhappy and complain about a situation and an environment we didn't like. To our credit, we hadn't been over the top in our complaints; we just didn't like it there.

"Go on," she commanded. "You can come back next weekend and visit your horses."

I was stunned. And livid. More than anything, I felt betrayed and abandoned. Why was she doing this to us? I would soon find out.

Dan powered up the ramp to the 91 freeway and continued his acceleration until he hit ninety miles per hour. I watched the speedometer from the back seat. He never slowed until he exited the freeway a half hour later. Along the way he told us this:

"Mom and Art are getting married."

They would be heading off to Las Vegas (a four-hour trip from Art's place) to marry and honeymoon, since apparently Art's divorce had just become final. Mom would return in a week to pick us up—and move us to Mira Loma permanently.

I want to say that this was the last straw, that hearing my brother say these things was hearing the last nail driven into the coffin of my sadness, sealing me into a depression that was like living death. I still remember the physical impact his words had on me. My body, of its own volition, slumped against the back seat. It no longer mattered that my brother was driving ninety miles an hour. In fact, some part of me wished he would simply lose control, which would bring my life and emotional anguish to an abrupt but welcome end. I want to say that this was the worst of it. Sadly, there was more heartache to come.

Mom and Art returned from Vegas several days later. I hadn't said anything to my friends about all this. In my heart, I was hoping against hope that Mom would return to say she'd had second thoughts, that they had decided to wait until Peg and I finished high school. But these thoughts were dashed as soon as they pulled up to the house and climbed out of Art's car, all smiles.

"Start packing," she told me. "We're moving to the ranch by the end of the week."

By "we" she meant herself, Peg and me. Dan, of course, had moved out long ago, and Kevin, our other brother, had graduated high school and would simply move in with friends rather than leave the area.

The guys in the neighborhood I rode bikes and horses with, my boyfriend Harold, my best friend Suzy—How could I leave them? These were the friends who had supported and sustained me in the years after my father died. We were all supposed to start high school together in two weeks. I couldn't imagine starting over in a new place, making all new friends.

At the same time, I'd been experiencing intense anxiety all week because we'd left our horses behind. Peg and I had always been the ones to feed and care for them. Here, they had a sturdy barn with box stalls where they would lounge in the heat of the day or take shelter during cold nights in winter. There, they were wandering around in a desolate field with no shelter at all in one hundred degree temperatures. Art didn't even do the feeding himself (which I suppose I was glad of, given his track record with his own horses). He paid an old man from a retirement home next door to feed our horses—a man who was a stranger to them.

I tried in vain to persuade my mother to see things from my perspective, to wait on the move for three years until I finished high school, but she shut me down unsympathetically with a terse, "You have your whole life ahead of you." While this statement was supposed to make me reflect on the wide world of opportunities just waiting for me around the bend, it pushed me further into depression. Why in heaven's name would I want to live in a world in which those closest to me, the ones who were supposed to care for and nurture me, abandoned and betrayed me?

My continuing physical weakness added to the emotional turmoil I was experiencing. I felt as though the blood in my veins had been replaced with lead. I moved heavily through the motions of putting the few possessions I had in bags and boxes. I have no memory at all of telling my friends good-by. At that point, I think I was still hoping I'd wake up and find it had all been a horrible nightmare.

We returned to the ranch mid-week. Rufus was there to meet us at the gate once again, and he tagged along at my heels as I headed straight for the "pasture" to see my horses.

"Go away, puppy," I told him bitterly when he tried to get my attention by jumping on me. I pushed him down, then wrapped my arms around my pony's neck as she nuzzled my back pockets, looking for carrots. I stayed with her until dinner time, Rufus coming and going, checking periodically to see if I was ready to give him some attention. Not yet.

As a quiet, introverted girl, I dreaded the thought of beginning in a new school without my friends, but I drew a small comfort from the fact that my out-going, assertive older sister would be there with me. Peg and I didn't share the same taste in much of anything— clothes, music, interests (except for our abiding love of animals) or personal style, and we often didn't see eye to eye on things. But push come to shove, she had always been there to watch over me when we were kids, and I counted on her to go before me into this new territory and pave the way.

My hopes for that evaporated the night before we were to begin at the new school.

The experiences of the previous year had taken their toll on my psyche, diminishing the shy but otherwise well-adjusted young girl and making me now sullen and fatalistic; I felt I had little control over the circumstances of my life, both immediate and future, and I had become simply resigned to my awful fate, much like a tortured captive. My sister, on the other hand, still maintained her strong, stubborn will.

Peg had spent the weekend hammering away at our mother, insisting that she be allowed to live with friends, like our brother, rather than go to a new high school. In her sophomore year, she had attended John F. Kennedy High School in Buena Park. She loved the school and her friends and the high school life. She'd tried out for cheer, preparing tirelessly beforehand, and though she hadn't made it, she'd come close, and was convinced that she could make the cheer squad in her junior year. No way did she intend to start over in a new school where no one knew her. Her approach with Mom was exactly as it had always been when she wanted something; she was insistent, demanding and absolutely relentless. Her incessant arguing finally reached its crescendo on Labor Day in the afternoon. We were set to begin school at Rubidoux High School the next day. ("I can't even pronounce it, much less spell it!" my sister had told me.) Peg and I would be walking to the corner and getting on a bus the next morning with no one we knew, riding to a city still foreign to us, and trying to find our way around a new campus.

But on the afternoon of our last day of summer, the four of us were seated around a rickety folding table outside. (The house on Art's property was not yet habitable, so we ate our meals outside under the big pepper tree, picking peppercorns from our plates when they fell.) Mom had made some mention of school the next day. Peg insisted that she wouldn't go to that school. In fact, she added, if Mom didn't allow her the same privilege Kevin had been given (of moving in with the family of friends), she would simply run away from home.

"I'll walk back to Orange County if you won't take me," she told our mother.

"Don't be ridiculous," Art interjected in a demeaning tone. I saw anger flash in my sister's eyes. To this point, Art had wisely opted to stay out of things, letting my mother deal with us. He and Peg had always gotten along surprisingly well. Now he was taking Mom's side. I settled back to watch the fireworks, never expecting what would happen next.

"I'm your father now, and I'm telling you this is the way it's going to be," Art continued.

Peg stood up.

"You're *not* my father," she told him.

Art stood. Then he slapped my sister across the face.

Decades have passed since this incident, yet I can still see it all vividly in my mind. Our father never,

ever hit us. If Peg or I needed disciplining, it was Mom who carried out the punishment. Our dad would never raise a hand to us.

After the initial shock that registered on her face, I was amazed at how quickly my sister composed herself.

"Then I disown you both as my parents," she said, and she turned and walked into the house. I followed her. The old house didn't have much more than our newly arrived bunk beds and dresser, but it did have a telephone. I watched, incredulous, as she dialed the operator. In minutes, she had a sheriff dispatched to the house. She put down the phone and walked outside to wait for him. Mom and Art were surprised, to say the least, when a cop car pulled into the yard about ten minutes later.

Peg immediately told the officer that she'd been abused by her step-father and wanted to be taken to a foster home.

There followed a half hour long conversation in which the calm, objective officer advised Art that hitting kids could get a person arrested and wasn't very wise parenting anyway, while also advising my sister that, like it or not, her "parents"—"He's *not* my *parent*," my sister spit back at him—had made a decision and we had no choice but to comply with their wishes.

"So you can't put me in a foster home?" Peg finally asked.

The patient officer explained again that foster homes were for extreme situations, telling her she'd have to be found to be "incorrigible" for that to happen.

"OK!" she said, as if agreeing to something. Then she turned and walked away.

Peg and I stayed up well past midnight talking. Her plan was to walk with me to the bus stop in the morning, as if she were really going to school, then head off down the road. She intended to walk to Norco (a distance of seven miles), then stand on the 91 freeway on-ramp with her thumb out. She was a pretty, sixteen-year-old girl. I would have successive nightmares that night, imagining all the horrible things that could happen to her.

We woke early, got dressed, and headed down to the bus stop. It was a strange moment. A few other kids were standing around, talking, when we walked up.

"Good luck," I told my sister.

"Don't worry, I'll get there," she told me. And then she walked away.

CHAPTER TWO

When Peg walked away from me at the bus stop, I felt as if I'd just been left by the side of the road in a strange town with no way to get back home. The bus would arrive any minute. I considered not getting on, just walking back home and making up some lie about missing it. I thought about running after Peg, telling her we'd go together. But I had always been the good kid, the one who followed the rules. Mom had said get on the bus. My conscience wouldn't let me openly defy her. I stood among the other kids at the stop, staring down at the ground. No one spoke to me. I spoke to no one. The bus pulled up and I got on, mercifully finding an empty seat so that I wouldn't have to sit by a stranger, and I could just stare out the window, wondering every minute where my sister was in her journey.

It was one of the longest days of my life. I remember little of what my new teachers said, except for my world history teacher, who mentioned casually that if students fell asleep in his class he failed them. "I show a movie every day," he said. "If you put your head down, I assume you're sleeping, and you'll receive an F at the semester." The boy in front of me turned halfway around in his seat and asked me to wake him if he ever fell asleep. He was the only person to speak to me through the course of the day.

Rufus, of course, met me at the gate when I returned, jumping and panting and wagging his tail. I ignored him as usual, brushing him aside as I walked up the driveway. There were no cars.

Art owned a small appliance repair shop in the city of Downey, and Mom worked for the school district in Long Beach, so when they'd decided to get married, they had agreed to commute together to work each day. Art would drop Mom off, then head to his shop, then pick her up again after work. It was a one hundred and twenty mile round trip every day, and they had to leave at 6:00 every morning to get Mom to work on time. On this day, however, Mom had opted to stay home from work. I think she suspected there might be a problem.

The house and trailer were deserted when I arrived home. Finally, I found a note. Mom had taken Peg down to our neighbors' in Orange County.

When she returned in the evening, Mom explained that Peg had been picked up—by the same officer who'd responded to the house the night before. His shift was just ending. He saw her walking and recognized her. When he brought her back, she told both him and our mother that she would continue to run away until she was taken back to Orange County. Mom called the Grays, our next-door-neighbors, and they agreed to allow Peg to stay with them during the school year. She'd come back to Art's on some weekends, various holidays and for the summer. And that was that.

I was happy for her, I envied her, and I'd never felt so alone in my life. Previously, the pattern of my life had been to walk home from school every day in the midst of a crowd of kids from my neighborhood, laughing and joking and looking forward to seeing our horses. We'd ride every day, Peg, Suzy, me and sometimes other kids we knew with horses. The pattern that developed in the days following Peg's escape was quite different. I'd ride the bus home, spend some time out back with the horses, then retreat to my room, sitting on the floor for hours listening to music. Late in the evening, Mom and Art would return home, often finding me still there, sitting in the dark. In those dark hours, I tried to envision a life ahead, after high school, after I'd turned eighteen and made my own escape. All I could see was a shadowy world in which good men were shot down for doing the right thing, there was little genuine love, and tenderness was nonexistent. I didn't want to live in such a world.

We were still living in turbulent times in terms of race relations. I had only been a student at Rubidoux High School for two weeks when race riots broke out on campus.

While I lived my life tucked deep inside my shell, there had been murmurings and undercurrents of unrest. On a Monday after school, I was one of the last kids to board the bus for Mira Loma. Seconds after I found a seat, something hit the window next to my head, then fell to the pavement and shattered. When I looked down to see a broken Coke bottle lying in the gutter, I realized that the bus was surrounded by black students. The kids who rode the bus from Mira Loma were mostly white, which I suppose was the reason we were targeted. Other objects began hitting the bus. The bus driver had shut the door, and she still gripped the long closing lever while a black student outside was trying to pry it open. Kids on the bus screamed at her to drive away, but she couldn't move forward without hitting someone, and now we could see that there were hundreds of black kids outside, smashing windows on cars, throwing trash cans, and attacking passersby. We watched in horror as a group of boys pulled a white student from his car and beat him senseless, leaving him lying in the street. Then we watched in amazement as a black student drove up, picked up the barely conscious young man, helped him into his car, and drove away. I would learn much later that the black student, James Cameron, a popular young man and a member of Rubidoux's football team, had driven the boy directly to a hospital in Riverside.

All around us, the violence teemed, while inside the bus, the screaming had reached a fever pitch. Only when some of the older boys threatened to commandeer the bus and drive us out of there did the bus driver begin inching forward. Thankfully, people in the crowd parted, though they continued to throw rocks and bottles at the bus until we were safely away.

My heart was still pounding a half hour later when I finally reached home, the sheer terror of the moment still fresh in my mind.

"What kind of school have you brought me to?" I demanded of my mother when she finally arrived home hours later. I told her all that had happened, but she expressed little concern. I remember Art chuckling and using a pejorative term in reference to the black students, one that would have earned me a smack from my mother had I chosen to use it. My parents had never been the model parents depicted in 1950's television shows, but one thing they had done right was to raise us color blind; they never made distinctions about people based on color or race.

While I could not convince my mother to return to the safety of Orange County, she did allow me to stay home from school for several days (mostly because I refused to get on the bus). For the remainder of the week, Mom and Art would rise early and leave for work by 6:00a.m. while I slept on. (I had begun to develop insomnia, often not falling asleep until 1:00 or 2:00 in the morning.) Later, when the sun was fully up and scorching through the curtainless windows of the dumpy house, I would get up, throw on some jeans, and wander around on Art's property.

Rufus became my constant shadow.

He still jumped up constantly, wanting to be petted. He was filthy from sleeping outside in the dirt, and one eye was constantly oozing from some kind of injury or infection. He would tag along until I stopped, then jump on me with muddy paws or rub his head on my leg, leaving long trails of goo from his runny eye. It didn't endear him to me.

And it was difficult for me to understand how Art seemed to want to keep him, but had no interest in his overall welfare. When Sandy was a puppy, we doted on her, taking her to the vet regularly for shots, check-ups and any other medical needs she had. Our parents' model had always been that of responsible pet owners. Art treated Rufus like a stray, yet he fed him along with the other dogs as if he belonged on the property.

I have to confess here that my disdain for my step-father colored everything. I was still sick, still depressed, still so angry and saddened by the loss of my friends and the hatred I'd seen in the world that I became bitter and hateful myself. I hated the house, the property, the high school, the town and all that came with it. And I hated Art. But for that, I had good reason.

I was twelve years old the first time Art tried to touch me inappropriately. He had started seeing my mother, though at the time I thought they were just friends. We were standing in his yard one day, and while he and Mom chatted away about something, Art reached over and put his hand on the back of my neck. I didn't like him very much even then; he was always drunk, and he didn't take care of his animals. But I tolerated him because I'd been taught to respect adults. I tried to ignore his hand on my neck. Art said something to Mom about getting them another couple beers, and she disappeared inside the house. His hand began moving slowly up and down my back.

Any woman who has had this happen as a young girl can describe a universal response. From this side of life, we wonder why we didn't haul back and kick the predator in the genitals, or at least administer a hard elbow to the chin. But generally the first response is really no response at all, since the shock of betrayal at the hands of someone trusted or familiar is usually enough to paralyze most girls, at least in the first moments. And men like Art are extremely subtle. He rubbed his hand slowly up and down my back as I stood there, awkward and uncomfortable, not knowing how to escape. Each time his hand moved roughly over my bra strap, he would giggle—"Hee hee hee"—in a high-pitched whisper.

"You like that, don't you?" he said quietly in my ear, adding that sinister chuckle I would quickly learn to loathe. "Over? Or under?"

Confused, I still wasn't responding. As Mom returned with a can of beer in each hand, I realized he'd been referring to my bra.

For the next three years, I tried to stay as far away from him as possible. Moving to the ranch put me in close proximity to him, and while I continued to avoid him, there were times when I couldn't escape.

Art owned a 1955 blue and white DeSoto sedan in gorgeous condition, a classic car from the 1950's which reminded me of my childhood. My boyfriend had taught me the rudiments of driving, and Art had seen me driving Mom's Impala up and down the long driveway at the ranch. One day, shortly after Peg and I had arrived for our "vacation" there, he offered to show me his car. He slid behind the wheel and told me to get in. I did, but left the passenger side door open. He told me that if I really liked the car, it could be mine someday. When I didn't respond, he offered to teach me how to drive a standard transmission. This tempted me—only because I was longing to find some means to escape. When I looked over at him, he patted his thighs, telling me that if I would just slide over and sit in his lap, he'd show me how easy it was. I got out of the car and walked away.

The little house that was on Art's property had only a toilet and a sink in the bathroom, so showers had to be taken in the trailer. After school started, I liked to take a shower in the evening so that I could sleep as late as possible in the morning. While Mom and Art were finishing dinner in the house, I would take my clean clothes and walk over to the trailer to shower. I was getting undressed one night when Art suddenly walked in.

"Just getting my cigarettes," he chuckled, as I scurried into the tiny bathroom and closed the door. I wondered, as I stood in the shower, why I hadn't heard the heels of his cowboy boots clomp up the wooden step before he suddenly appeared in the trailer.

The next night it happened again, only this time I was fully dressed, waiting for him. I had barely heard him tip toe up the step. While he got his cigarettes, I simply stood glaring at him, arms folded across my chest. He giggled, then ducked out the door, and I made a show of locking it behind him.

After my shower, I waited for a chance to talk to Mom alone, then demanded angrily, "Could you keep your husband in the house with you when I go out to shower? I don't really appreciate it when he purposely walks in on me while I'm getting dressed." I wanted to shock her. I wanted her to be repulsed by this man she'd married who was some kind of pervert trying to peep at her adolescent daughter. Instead, Mom responded with anger in return.

"Don't be ridiculous," she said, using Art's pet phrase. "You don't have anything for him to see anyway."

From my adult perspective now, I can easily attribute my mother's response to two separate dynamics. First, there was the denial, a common defense mechanism which is frequently seen in women who cannot accept the awful truth that a man they love might be deviant. And dovetailing on the denial was the insidious insult—I wasn't desirable anyway. I have grown up under my mother's constant criticism and ongoing resentment, and, while her reasons are not worth going into here, I do understand them—now.

But back then I was an emerging young woman, just fifteen. I needed an advocate, someone to be on my side, to be enraged by Art's behavior and to do something to protect me and allow me to feel safe again. Instead, I was reprimanded.

"Art said you locked him out of the trailer," she accused, glaring at me.

"I *did* lock the door," I replied, "after he—"

"Well, don't do it again," she cut me off. "That's where he lives, and if he needs something, he has to be able to get in there."

And that was that.

Before this time, I had been adrift in a sea of sadness. Now it felt as if cruel hands were slowly pushing me beneath the surface, deeper and deeper, the light fading, the cold intensifying. I found it difficult to breathe.

From that point forward, I had to be on my guard constantly. I would shut off the lights in the house at night and get in bed only to hear, moments later, the back door open (another door I was not allowed to lock, though I slept in the house alone), and Art's boots scuffling furtively across the kitchen floor. Sometimes he would simply stand there in the dark, waiting, listening, as I waited, listened. I always let him know in some way that I was awake—coughing, sneezing, clearing my throat loudly and defiantly, sometimes even singing. Eventually he would creep off again. I took to sleeping in my clothes, and I never let myself fall asleep until I was relatively certain he was in his trailer for the night.

In retrospect, I realize that I never feared Art. I never had to endure the horrors some other young girls have been subjected to at the hands of predatory men. While I felt uncomfortable around him at all times, and I was disgusted by him in every way, he never threatened me, never attempted to force me. I think he knew instinctively, once we were sharing the same living space, that I was prepared to fight back. As I'd grown older, he had ceased the overt attempts at fondling me, but continued taking every opportunity to see what he could see. Despite my constant vigilance, hearing his boots at times scuff the gravel outside my bedroom window at night would make my heart pound with fury. In the daylight, the sight of Art, the very thought of him, made my stomach clench in disgust.

And since Rufus was on the property when we arrived, I could only associate him with Art. In my mind, he was part of the man I loathed, as ugly and annoying as the man himself, and I didn't want to have anything to do with him.

But that dog just wouldn't leave me alone.

The weekend after the riots, I was told that I would be returning to school on Monday. Mom and Art had been reading about the situation in the local newspaper, and they assured me that everything had "calmed down" at the high school now, and it was safe to return.

Monday morning I awoke with a feeling of horrible dread. I pulled on jeans, sandals, and a blouse, and at the last moment possible, began my trudge down the driveway toward the bus stop. Rufus followed me. I stopped at the gate.

"Stay here," I said, shaking my finger at him. He just looked at me and wagged his tail. I started to walk through the gate and he tried to follow me again, so I closed the big chain link gates which usually stayed open. I walked toward the corner and Rufus followed along the fence line. When I reached the end of Art's property, I heard him whimpering. I kept walking. Then I heard the loud rattle of chain link, and suddenly Rufus was bounding toward me, wagging his tail.

"*Go home, you stupid dog!*" I scolded. He ignored me, happy to be out in the early morning sunshine, trotting ahead and sniffing, then coming back to join me. If I took him back, I'd miss the bus. If I missed the bus, Mom and Art would never believe it wasn't intentional. I ignored the dog and followed my fate to the bus stop.

"Is that your dog?" one of the girls on the corner asked. It was the first time any of that group had addressed me directly.

"Um, sort of," I mumbled.

"What's his name?" she asked.

"Uh, Rufus," I replied. A loud twitter of laughter erupted from the group.

"He's just my step-father's stupid dog," I said, annoyed. "Go *home*," I said to Rufus, to further detach myself. He ignored me, of course, and continued to trot around, sniffing at everything—rocks, weeds, fences—and peeing on everything he sniffed. When he started sniffing kids' backpacks, I had a horrible moment of fright. If he peed on one, I'd be mortified. As if I wasn't already.

The bus came.

"Go *home*," I told him one more time, even though I knew he had no idea what I was saying. Really, it was just for the sake of the other kids there. I didn't know what to do. I had to get on the bus, but my dog—I mean, Art's dog—was out of the yard, a hundred yards from home. Once again I felt I had no choice other than to climb the steps of the bus and let fate play out its hand. As the bus pulled away from the corner, I saw Rufus through the window, trotting in the direction of Art's place.

Arriving at school was one of the more surreal experiences of my life. SWAT officers stood on the roofs of the buildings. They were in an 'at ease' posture, but they were holding shotguns.

It's hard to imagine any school board or parent group these days standing still for police officers armed with shotguns hovering over their children. But back then we seemed to believe the adage that "might makes right," and intimidation, if not downright brutalization, was the rule.

I went through ghost classes that day—some with only substitute teachers, most with high levels of absenteeism. The teachers who were present assigned very little work, which was small compensation for all the ugliness.

After school, there were very few kids on the bus, so I had a seat all to myself, but I didn't begin to relax until the bus was several blocks away from the school.

Reaching home, I found Rufus at the gate to meet me, as always. And I found Bill, the old man who fed Art's horses.

"That dog got out of the yard today," his gravelly voice proclaimed as he pointed a crooked, arthritic finger at Rufus. "He climbed right over the chain link fence! I saw him!"

Apparently Bill had been in the yard next door and he'd seen the dog take a running leap, jump onto the fence where it triangulated in the corner, then scramble up and over. The fence was four feet high, but it had loosened with age and was definitely already sagging in that spot.

For some reason, I suddenly felt defensive.

"He followed me to the bus stop," I said. Rufus was leaning against my leg, rubbing his bad eye on my jeans. I set my hand lightly on his dirty head as I looked at the old man in defiance.

"Dogs need to stay in the yard," Bill snapped, then turned and shuffled away.

That night when Mom and Art arrived home from work, Bill hurried over from next door to tattle on Rufus. I could hear him talking to Art as they stood in the driveway.

"Why does he care?" I muttered aloud. "Nosey old man."

At dinner, the issue was raised, and I was told not to allow Rufus to follow me.

"How am I supposed to stop him?" I asked, incredulous as I realized I was being blamed.

"Tell him to go home," Art told me.

"I *did* tell him," I replied, which prompted my mother to say my name in a cautionary tone.

"What?" I demanded. "He's not *my* dog. I don't have any control over what he does. If you cared about him at all, you'd train him." That last bit, directed at Art, got me sent away from the table. We were finally eating indoors these days, and the old wooden floorboards of the house boomed as I stormed into my bedroom.

The next day, Rufus followed me again, repeating the routine from the day before, barking and whining as I locked the big gates, then simply running along the fence line and jumping the fence.

He followed me to school every day that week. After a few days, the other kids at the bus stop were calling him by name, petting him, and telling me how cool it was that he walked me to the bus every day.

Every evening, the issue was discussed at dinner, with the implication that I was purposely calling him out of the yard to walk with me. I didn't care what Art thought, but I couldn't convince my mother this wasn't true. In taking Art's side, she was basically calling me a liar, which was one more betrayal I found devastating.

On Friday, I came home from school depressed, weary, and on the verge of collapse, both physically and emotionally. While kids at school talked about all they had to look forward to on the weekend, I had nothing. I missed my boyfriend, and I knew that he would be spending the weekend hanging out with friends. He had a car, but he didn't have a job, as he was still in high school, so gas money was an issue, in addition to his parents not allowing him to drive so far. Peg would be having a great weekend with friends as well. She'd recently joined a church youth group, and every weekend now meant being involved in fun activities with other teens. I would be stuck at "the ranch" with Mom and Art, where I was under constant criticism for my bad attitude and refusal to "get along."

I opened a Dr. Pepper and went outside to sit on the back step in the sun and try to think of a way out of the shitty mess that was my life, knowing that when Mom and Art returned home from work, I'd be scolded again for "letting" Rufus get out of the yard.

Of course, he was right there, pushing his head against me, trying to get me to play with him.

"Leave me alone," I told him, shoving him away. He came right back. I shoved him again, to no avail. I picked up a rock.

"Go fetch!" I told him, throwing the rock as far as I could. And he did. Gravel flew everywhere as he took off after the rock, bringing me back the very one I'd thrown, though the yard and driveway were littered with stones. He dropped it at my feet.

"It's a rock, you stupid dog!" I shouted the words at him with all the force behind my pent up anger. He simply sat down expectantly, wagging his tail. Guilt flooded my veins like saltwater, stinging me from the inside out. I looked at him—really looked at him—for the first time. None of this was his fault. He'd been abandoned, left behind, and Art had kept him only because he couldn't be bothered to do anything else with him. It wasn't his fault that he was dirty and ill mannered; no one had given him the attention he needed because, up until that point, no one had cared about him. I felt the same way.

"It's OK, Ruf," I told him, patting his head. He leaned his dusty body against my knees and sighed as a patient dog will. He would forgive my rude and irascible behavior toward him as if it had never existed. Because that's what dogs do. It is their nature to forgive—and forget. I put my arms around his neck and hugged him.

Over dinner that night, the conversation arose again about keeping Rufus in the yard, with Art now threatening to chain him up, a practice I find appalling. I started to argue, but decided to keep my cool and make a plea for the dog's welfare. I talked to Mom about his eye, reminding her that Rufus had never had any vaccinations, and that, if he were going to stay on the property, he needed to be licensed—especially considering his habit of getting out of the yard. It might have been her guilt that caused her to acquiesce, but she told me that if I could find a vet who had Saturday hours, we'd take him the next day. It took me less than two minutes with a phone book to find a place in Rubidoux, a block from the high school.

Ruf behaved well at the vet's office the next day, even when it came to his eye examination, which included a minor surgical procedure. As it turned out, he had a small foxtail under his lower eyelid. For weeks, the dog had been rubbing his eye on every human he encountered, trying to let us know that something wasn't right. He couldn't help himself, and he was trying to ask us to relieve him of the pain and irritation, which we just found irritating ourselves. Poor Ruf. Humans, from my perspective, tend to be poor listeners. The eye had become inflamed and infected, and I felt like the biggest jerk in the world when the vet asked how long it had been that way. We deserved far worse than the doctor's look of disapproval. But guilt is a powerful motivator. We came home from the vet's office with medication for Ruf's eye, and I never missed a dosage. In days, the infection had healed.

We still had the issue of him following me to the bus stop every day. For awhile, Art got in the habit of chaining Ruf up every morning when he left for work—and I was told I'd be grounded if I made good on my threat to unchain him the minute they left every day. I laughed at that. Grounded? I had nowhere to go and no one to see. The plan was to have Bill unchain the dog after we'd all left for the day. They tried it for awhile, but when Bill reported back to Art that the minute the dog was off the chain, he ran for the corner, scaled the fence and went looking for me, they gave up. Finally, Ruf was allowed to escort me to the bus stop every morning and see me off safely—as if he were the protective father and I the small child—because he always immediately returned home, and because Art had long ago lost the battle of wills with him.

And it was a good thing he had. Several weeks later, I finally felt strong enough to ride again. As I saddled up Billy, a tall bay gelding I'd procured through some creative horse trading and exchange of funds, Ruf trotted around, sniffing the horsie smells of hoof cleanings and tail combings, and while he did I explained that he wouldn't be able to go with me. When I left in a car, Ruf understood that he couldn't go with me. He would follow the car—my mom's Impala or Art's old truck—to the gate, but stop as we drove away. He never tried to follow. I hoped he would do the same as I left on Billy.

When I rode through the big chain link gate, I closed it without dismounting.

"Stay," I commanded Rufus, who sat on the other side, wagging his tail. I tried to urge Billy into a quick walk as I headed away, but it wouldn't have mattered if I'd charged off at a gallop. I hadn't even made it past Art's property line before I heard the chain link rattle and saw Rufus scrambling over the fence, this time in the opposite corner from where he'd been getting out to walk me to the bus.

"Ruf!" I said, exasperated. He trotted up beside Billy, looked up at me reproachfully for trying to ditch him, then trotted on ahead, taking his place as lead scout. I sighed. Then I resigned myself to his company. Either Art would build a taller fence to keep him in, or Rufus would be my constant riding companion. It turned out to be the latter.

CHAPTER THREE

The hot California September days had turned to cooler autumn days by this time, and I rode often. Somehow, getting out of the house and away from Art's property was a small respite from the constant tension and sadness associated with that place.

Because I was still trying to maintain a relationship with my boyfriend in Orange County, I would take a trip to the Mira Loma post office every day after school. I'd been told I could never call Harold as it was long distance. (This was in the days before cell phones existed, of course. I really believe Mom felt if she could sever my OC ties, I'd resign myself to living in the Riverside area. How little she understood about the enduring passion of teen romance.) I'd gotten in the habit of writing Harold a letter every day (which gave me something to do during those ghost classes). I would come home from school, shove my daily letter in an envelope, then either walk or ride Billy up to the post office, with Rufus always by my side.

Ducking into the building through a side door, I would drop my letter, and be out again within seconds, while Ruf sat waiting by the door patiently. This was not a trained behavior. I never told him to stay.

He never ran off, and I never worried about him being off leash just steps away from the parking lot. When I look back on it now, it still amazes me that nothing awful ever happened to him. Well, except once....

One day, I had to buy stamps, which changed the course of my routine. Rufus and I had walked to the post office, but though I'd come in through the side door as usual, I went around to the front desk to make my purchase. I was in a pretty deep funk that day; I hadn't seen Harold for weeks, and though I wrote him every day, he never wrote me back. My sister had assured me that he missed me terribly every day. I had also been writing to Peg, and she replied to my letters, with plenty of news about the neighborhood—including the fact that she was keeping in touch with Harold. He missed me so much, according to her, that he was "sad" every day, and he stopped by Suzy's house often to ask Peg to relay messages to me. But he couldn't seem to find the time or make the effort to write a few words on a piece of paper and send it off to me. Love is truly blind....

With the heavy mantle of loneliness weighting me down that day, I shuffled out the front door of the post office, head down, lost in thought, leaving Rufus behind. It wasn't until I arrived home twenty minutes later—and he didn't come bounding toward the gate to greet me—that I realized I'd left him behind. Had I been in better physical condition, I would have run all the way back. At my best, I was an underweight, asthmatic kid. Still suffering the effects of my protracted illness, I was usually exhausted just walking the half mile to the post office and back every day. Now I was going back a second time, and I couldn't make my body move fast enough. Finally, I crossed the main street through Mira Loma and ran up the steps and around to the side of the post office. There was Ruf, lying on the cement steps by the side door, still waiting patiently. What a dog. I threw my arms around his neck and apologized over and over for making him wait so long. Once again I was amazed that this dog could be so loyal, so committed to me, when most of the humans in my life had let me down.

And that included Harold. Ironically, I had only met him because my sister had decided she didn't want to be his girlfriend. They had met at a party one night, and were together for the duration of the evening. But the next day when Harold had come looking for her, Peg told me to go the door and tell him she wasn't home. That's how we met. Days later we went riding together, and Harold began to hang around with my group of friends. Within weeks, we were a couple. We'd been together for a year when the horrible summer of 1969 began. I had always thought Harold's level of commitment matched mine, but looking back, after I'd been bedridden for months, then having moved so far away, he no doubt wanted to move on, but would have felt like a jerk if he'd added one more cut to my plethora of wounds. Harold had a tough guy exterior—he was a cowboy, after all—but he had always been gentle and careful with me, which is why I loved him so much. He had been the only source of tenderness in my life since my father died, and I clung to him because of it. But he, too, seemed fated to disappoint me.

I suppose I was not surprised when I came home from school one day and opened the mailbox to find a letter from Peg detailing how Harold had recently stopped by, had stayed to talk to her for hours, how one thing had led to another. He was human, he needed affection, she just happened to be the one there to comfort him, and so on. The empty words told the tale.

The next and final letter I wrote to him let him know that I forgave him, and that he was free to see whomever he chose.

Before my break-up with Harold, I had been depressed. But my relationship with him had been the one faint ray of light at the end of a very dark, very cold tunnel. Like Ariadne's string in a labyrinth of abandonment and betrayal, I'd held onto the tenuous hope that time would pass, he'd get a job or I'd get my driver's license, some-how we'd start making trips to see each other, and even-tually everything would be alright. I knew none of that would happen now, and I was left with an emptiness like nothing I'd ever felt before. I would lie awake for hours at night, trying to make sense of it all, and wanting more than anything for my life to simply end.

We always wish, when we finally get our grown-up eyes, that we could have a 'do-over' of our childhood. Now that I have raised four children myself, I can see my parents as humans, not as gods, struggling to negotiate the obstacle course of life while more chal-lenges are being thrown at them sideways.

My parents never planned my birth, and it was clear to everyone as I grew up that they had not welcomed it. Dad had always wanted a daughter. They had a son, then another one. Finally my mother gave birth to a girl, and my father was elated. Eighteen months later, I was born. My siblings were blonde-haired, blue-eyed, porcelain-skinned cherubs. I was a green-eyed brunette with very dark olive skin tones. The truth is, I simply didn't fit anywhere in my family. These words do not emanate from a place of teen-aged angst. I am looking across the decades from the comfort of self love and acceptance to see the reality of my family dynamic. My father doted on my sister and had no time and little love left for me. My mother resented her "diaphragm baby" (which is how she introduced me to strangers) and even as a small child, I could sense her irritation when I tried to get close to her. Hence, my instinctive need to make myself invisible, to fade into the background and play the role of observer, not participant, in my family.

Simply put, Harold had made me feel wanted. In giving me his time, attention, and gentle, innocent affection, he had made me feel as if I really meant something important to someone, as if I mattered in the world. All the loneliness of my childhood had been erased by the long hours we'd spent riding horses together or listening to music and just goofing around.

Now all that loneliness returned and was intensified by my isolation in Mira Loma. There was no one to whom I could turn, no affection offered from any source. In fact, I felt my mother's resentment and irritation at my presence more so than I ever had before, and the truth is, had I not been around, things would have been much easier for her in her new marriage.

I fantasized often about what it would mean to take my own life. I'd been raised Catholic, but that background amounted to no more than meaningless ritual for me. Every night when I climbed into bed, the sorrows of my life descended upon my psyche like demons. Every morning when I awoke, I dreaded getting up, moving through the day, my soul exposed to more abuse.

And the abuse certainly came. Once Art knew that I had told my mother about his attempts to leer at me, he became viciously hostile. He started imposing rules about what I could or could not do. If I protested, I was sent to my room. While she may not have done everything right, Mom had always acknowledged the importance of the horses in our lives, and had rarely placed restrictions on our time with them. Art, however, saw this as an opportunity for revenge, and was constantly punishing me by telling me I couldn't ride or couldn't spend time with the horses. Once, when I was out in the pasture, Art appeared out of nowhere and began to criticize me for the way I was bridling my horse, telling me to stop immediately and do things his way. I ignored him. The next thing I knew, I was on the ground. He had kicked me hard in the tailbone with the toe of his boot, sending pain like electric shockwaves up my spine. For a few terrifying minutes, I didn't think I could move my legs. But the adrenaline released by my anger at him gave me the strength to stand, and I somehow managed to walk away.

Physical wounds, with time, will usually heal. Psychological wounds, on the other hand, may fester for decades if not treated. Certainly the worst scars inflicted on me by my step-father were the latter kind. I had always tried to ignore him. Now I would not speak to him unless I had to, which enraged him. His retaliation was to call me names and belittle me.

"You know you really are homely, aren't you?" he said one night as I tried to step around him to get to the kitchen. As I stood at the sink to do the dishes, he went on to tell me I was skinny, flat-chested and shaped like a boy.

"Art," Mom said half-heartedly from the other room. It was the closest she'd ever come to defending me.

"What?" he replied like a petulant child. "I'm just telling her the truth." He gave his derisive laugh.

Had I grown up with a more positive self-image, I would have thought his insults were absurd and laughable. Sadly, I believed every word he said. When I page through the diary I kept back then, I read nothing but words of bitterness and self-loathing. At that age, we simply cannot be objective about ourselves. I saw myself only through the eyes of those who abandoned, belittled and rejected me. I thought that people were right not to care about me; there was little about me that anyone would value.

Except for Ruf. I was the center of his universe. I would lie awake at night for hours, finally falling asleep after 1:00a.m., then somehow wake at 6:30 to get ready for school. Art had a rule about animals in the house. He refused to allow Rufus to set foot inside the door, and Ruf was wise to keep to those boundaries. As soon as I made it to the kitchen in the morning, though, he would jump on the back door, his large paws leaving dirt streaks as he peered in through the window, wagging his tail. When I stepped outside to head for the bus stop, he was ecstatic, running up and down the gravel drive and bringing me things—rocks, sticks, hoof trimmings—to throw for him, which I did. I was cloaked in sadness, but somehow his antics made me smile.

I don't know why I kept going to school every day. One or two kids had gotten to know me because I was the new girl and they were curious, but I really hadn't nurtured any friendships. In the back of my mind, I just didn't see myself living there permanently. And I certainly wasn't learning anything. But I went through the motions, more to escape Art's wrath than for any other reason, and I looked forward always to the moment when I would reach the gate after school, calling out to Ruf, who would come running to meet me.

That winter was long and cold and dark. Art's house had only a small floor furnace in the living room, so I was cold most of the time. Rufus had made himself a kind of shallow den in the dirt beside the house as close to the back door as he could get, and I put a carpet remnant down with an old blanket so he could at least have some warmth. It didn't help much when it was pouring rain outside.

The subject of Ruf being kept outside in all weather was one more issue I found myself arguing about with Art. I tried reasoning with him, appealing to Mom— nothing worked. Art had been raised on a farm in Nebraska, and in his mind, dogs were meant to be kept outside with the livestock, not brought into the house to be "pampered." I knew it was useless to fight with him, but it was one battle in which I refused to surrender, even though I knew the outcome before I ever began. Very little in my life had any meaning or worth at that point, except for that dog.

Ruf and I had become inseparable.

Looking back, I know I would not have survived that winter without him. Those were the darkest days of my life. I felt angry and betrayed, cut off from most of my family and all of my friends. Once I became clinically depressed, I began to focus on only one issue: escape from the constant, abiding sadness. Alone at night in my bed, my thoughts whirled incessantly around ending my life. But I couldn't abandon Ruf. He was my guardian and companion, my only source of love and affection. I couldn't bear the thought of leaving him to his fate with Art. So I somehow found the courage every morning to get up and plod through the day, wearing the mantle of my grief upon my shoulders.

But time brings change, and as the days finally moved into summer, my life changed in several ways. The days grew longer and warmer. School ended. My sister returned to Art's to stay for the summer, and we became united against a common enemy. And, most critical in terms of my recovery from depression, I passed my driver's test two weeks after my sixteenth birthday. The year had changed me in terms of my personality; I had gone from a happy teenager who loved her boyfriend to a sullen, cynical young woman who no longer trusted anyone. But getting my driver's license meant that, at least on occasion, I could get behind the wheel of my mother's Chevy Impala and drive away from everything—everyone—that hurt me.

Those occasions to drive grew more frequent that summer as Mom's relationship with her husband began to deteriorate. More and more, Art distanced himself from her, leaving her at home for long hours on the weekends while he went off to ride horses or drink with his friends or both. The colder he became, the harder she tried to make the marriage work. So while my life had become less lonely with the companionship of my sister and having my mom off work for the summer, my mother was now the one feeling the sting of abandonment and rejection. Whether it was out of guilt or empathy or both, she began letting me drive her car nearly every time I asked.

On one hot midsummer's evening, Peg and I drove to the local drive-in movie theater and saw Disney's "Aristocats." Before the film, we sat in the car talking about how much had changed, and how life would be different now that I could drive. Peg encouraged me to put the pressure on Mom, to insist she allow me to move back to Orange County, to run away—taking the car—if Mom refused. I know she interpreted my quiet demeanor as agreement, but in my heart I knew I would never follow such a plan, even if it meant returning to my friends and escaping from the constant fear of being alone with Art. I would have to leave my horses behind if I left Mira Loma. Worse, I would have to leave Ruf, and I couldn't do that. I knew that when school started again in September, Peg would return to Orange County, Mom would return to work, and I would be alone again. In the meantime, I just tried to make the most of that summer.

Peg and I rode horses or went for walks. She was teaching me to play guitar, so sometimes we'd sit for hours under the big pepper tree and play chords or sing folk songs. Whatever we did, wherever we went, Ruf was with us, trotting along beside or running ahead or flopping down in the dirt at my feet.

Eventually he began going along on the car rides as well. If we didn't take him, he jumped the fence and ran alongside the road for fifty yards or so, eventually turning back to head home. One day I pulled over and coaxed him into the car with us. After that, he nearly always went along.

His practice of riding in the car with me would enable him to save me from an assault. But it would also be the way I would eventually come to lose him.

That summer of newfound freedom ended far too quickly, and Peg headed back to start her senior year of high school at Kennedy. Instead of returning to work, though, Mom had decided to take an early retirement. I think she believed that if she worked hard enough at being the good wife, she could win Art's affection again. But it was clear that he'd had his fill of having the wife and kids around all the time, and his interests lay only in drinking, not in nurturing relationships. While I was at school during the day, Mom worked on the little shack of a house, scraping wallpaper, patching, painting and trying to make it livable. She would enlist my help in the afternoon, only stopping to make Art some elaborate dinner and have it on the table when he came home from work. Night after night I watched him push his chair back from the table and head for his trailer to go to bed, leaving her alone to do the dishes and clean up.

The tension between them was palpable.

And it was worse on the weekends, when Art was home all day. I tried to be gone as often as I could, riding for long hours away from home.

I had traded Billy, my stocky bay gelding (who was a good saddle horse, but not much of a friend) for Topaz, a dusky young mare with spirit and grace. Her previous owners hadn't done much with her, as they'd been afraid of her frisky behavior, so I had undergone the project of training her from the ground up—bridle to saddle to rider. By the end of the summer, she was a fleet, sure-footed trail horse. She loved to run, so I would take her down to the Santa Ana River bottom where there were long stretches of shallow sand. All I had to do was drop the reins and lean forward and she was off. Forty years later, I can still remember what it was like to be on her back at a full gallop.

Rufus would tear along the sand beside her, doing his best to keep up. When he slowed, I reined her in, and we would walk, then rest, along the river. Topaz had one fear—water—and it took me months to get her to walk in it. But Ruf loved it, and he'd splash around like a little kid, chasing after the rocks I threw for him, sometimes diving underwater to emerge with the exact rock I'd tossed. He was my clown, my entertainment, my personal jester who took the job of making me smile quite seriously. And it was truly a tough job, as I still found little to smile about.

Then came the evening when his role turned from clown to guardian in a heartbeat.

One of the many transitions I found difficult in moving from Orange County to Mira Loma was adjusting to living in a rural setting. In Cypress, we had lived within bicycling distance of Disneyland, Knott's Berry Farm, and the ocean. In Mira Loma, we had to drive ten miles just to get to a supermarket, which was five miles outside of the closest large city, Riverside. But with my license, I could be in Riverside in a matter of twenty minutes. Often in the evenings, especially on weekends, I would borrow Mom's car and drive into the city, just to walk the long outdoor mall on the warm nights of Indian summer.

Of course, Rufus always went with me, and he was never on a leash. Back then, there was a series of fountains along the mall which had been created to resemble outdoor scenes, with grassy knolls and water running over rocks. Ruf and I would walk along the mall, looking in the windows of the shops that were closed for the day, stopping from time to time so Ruf could splash in the tumbling water.

There were no street lights in Mira Loma and no sidewalks. Walking alone along the streets at home would have been dangerous, but little did I know how vulnerable I was while walking in the lighted mall alone at night in Riverside.

Nowadays kids often walk with their heads down, texting on their phones or equally distracted by the music in their ears. For me, it was my contemplative nature that kept me looking always inward instead of noticing my surroundings. The young man's arm snaked around my waist before I'd had time to realize someone was beside me.

"Hey baby," he said. "There's a party at my place right now. Wanna come?"

I was wearing a midriff top with hip-hugger jeans, the prevalent '60's style. I could feel his fingers pressing into the bare skin at my rib cage.

"No thanks," I muttered, trying to fake a polite tone. "I need to get—"

"What's your hurry?" he asked, with no pretense of politeness as he pulled my body toward him, his hand tightening as it slid up under my breast. I could feel the taut muscles in his arm hold fast as I tried to pull back. I was five feet, five inches tall and weighed just over a hundred pounds, a slip of a girl against a man who was nearly twice my weight and a head taller. My mind raced as I tried not to panic. Years before in a terrifying ordeal when a prowler had broken into a home where I was staying, I'd learned how our fight or flight response can shut down our cognitive abilities, paralyze our ability to speak... or scream.

Suddenly I lost my balance and would have fallen if the man had not been clutching me so tightly. He had attempted to drag me down the sidewalk, but I tripped over something. Someone. Rufus. He had squeezed his body between us. I looked down to see the hair on his back raised. He emitted a low, menacing growl. I had never seen either of these behaviors in this goofy jester of a dog before, and I was probably just as startled as my would-be attacker, who quickly released his hold and stepped backward.

"Uh... Your dog doesn't bite, does he?" he stammered, still taking backward steps, his eyes on Rufus.

"Only when he meets bad people," I managed to say as I slid my fingers beneath Ruf's collar as if to hold him back. He was still watching the man, still growling.

Rufus and I stood staring as the man hurried off down the sidewalk, then vanished into a dark alley. The minute he disappeared, my fierce protector, with one full-body shake of his fur, morphed back into his normal clownish demeanor, wagging his tail and jumping up to try and lick my face. For once, I didn't discourage his behavior. My heart was pounding and my hands were shaking, but I knelt on the sidewalk to hug my dog and thank him for saving me from whatever fate that creep had intended for me. Then we ran to the car together. I made Ruf sit next to me all the way home so I could keep one arm around him as I drove, to help me calm down.

I never told anyone about that night, or at least, not the whole story. I was too embarrassed by my stupidity and naiveté, and I knew if Mom ever found out, my trips to downtown Riverside at night would end. As it was, I limited my gallivanting to the early evening hours after that, heading home before dark—and I never went down there alone again. I always took Ruf as my bodyguard. It seems an understatement to say he was more than just a companion to me, and perhaps only those who've been friends with a dog in this way can understand; I felt closer to Ruf than I did to anyone else in my life. He loved me unconditionally. He was completely and utterly devoted to me. He was genuinely happy to be with me, no matter what kind of mood I was in. And I knew he would guard me with his life. I loved him more deeply than I had ever loved anyone.

CHAPTER FOUR

That winter was not as lonely for me as the previous one had been. I had made some friends at school, and sometimes we talked on the phone at night or I drove over to see them—always with Rufus. I spent a lot of time playing my guitar or listening to music. And I kept out of Art's way.

As he'd grown distant from Mom, he'd left off all pretense of trying to get along with me in front of her. Now his criticism and cruel remarks were constant. I managed to avoid him most of the time, but Mom still insisted we all have dinner together, and it was always the worst half hour of my day. Like many American families in the '70's, we often ate dinner with the television tuned to the evening news—and the news back then centered around the war in Vietnam. I had found myself being drawn back into the drama of politics, guided once again by a great teacher, Kent Campbell, my U.S. History teacher. I had strong opinions about our government's involvement in Vietnam, but I quickly learned not to voice them over dinner. Art ridiculed, mocked or scorned any topic I brought up, from politics to music to horse training. Eventually, our meals were silent requiems with the sights and sounds of a horrific war as background.

We were not a family. We were reluctant, resentful roommates. The tension between us had become explosive. One night, with a small spark, it simply ignited.

I don't remember what was said at dinner, but at some point Art became angry and stormed out of the house. As fortune would have it, my brother had come up to stay with us for a few days, so he was there with me. When Art walked out, Mom stayed inside with us—until we heard his car start. She went outside to see where he was going, to try to talk to him, and we could hear them arguing outside. Kevin and I went to a window so that we could hear what was being said. Mom was speaking in quiet, calm tones, as if she were talking to a child, trying to get Art to come inside and talk to her about their relationship. He flatly refused over and over, telling her, "Move out of the goddamn way or I'll run you down." I thought about calling the police, but I knew both of them would be furious with me if I did. Kevin agreed and said that if he went outside and tried to interfere, it would only make Art angrier. I stood by the window, biting my nails, my stomach churning, confused and conflicted about what to do. Then we heard my mother cry out, and Kevin headed for the door. I stood peering out the window into the darkness. I could see Mom sitting on the dirt and gravel driveway, rubbing her arm. She would tell me later that she had tried to step in front of him and Art had pushed her to the ground. My loathing of him increased tenfold. The situation would have escalated, I'm sure, but Kevin's presence outside convinced them to retreat to their separate corners.

They ignored each other for days, during which time my mother apparently filed for divorce and found another place for us to live. I came home from school one day to learn that she and Art would be separating. Before I could ask, she explained that we wouldn't be moving back to Cypress just yet; the tenants in our home there had a one-year lease, which wouldn't be up until the end of the summer—still six months away. She'd purchased a tiny two-bedroom house— with horse corrals—a couple of miles away, so that, as soon as the sale closed escrow, we could move out, taking our horses with us.

Life had taken a decided turn for the better, it seemed. That sensation lasted only seconds. She went on to tell me that when she had revealed her plan to Art, he had told her to "go ahead and go," but that we couldn't take Rufus with us.

Each year when I teach *The Tragedy of Romeo and Juliet* to my high school freshmen, I try to help them understand the depth of Romeo's emotion. Imagine how he felt, I tell them, having isolated himself from family and friends, an insomniac who was so sad he couldn't bear the light of day and would roam the woods at night. Suddenly he is rescued from his miasma of depression by someone whose love and devotion matches his own intensity of feeling—only to be told, within hours of pledging his love to her, that he must leave forever and cannot take her with him. Most teenagers have been taught that suicide is "stupid" and a coward's way out, but they understand Romeo's subsequent desperation in a way that few adults can, as they have not yet learned to shield their young and vulnerable hearts.

I didn't want to believe that my step-father was capable of such cruelty, yet I knew that it was true. I had seen him interact with horses, with my own young mare, in fact, when she wouldn't load into a trailer because she was frightened. On that day, he'd wrapped a chain around her nose and jerked it again and again until it opened a raw and bleeding wound. When he had her trembling with pain and fear, he dragged her up the ramp, then chuckled at his success and my tears. Her nose was scarred for life, as was her heart and mine. I knew that he would keep Rufus to spite me for rejecting and defying him. I was, as Romeo himself declared, "Fortune's fool," and the heartbreak was such that I found myself once again contemplating suicide.

In the weeks prior to our moving out, the only ray of hope I clung to was my mother's insistence that we would fight for Rufus when they went to court to have the marriage dissolved. Sadly, I had learned to distrust her, so I suspected this was something she told me in order to keep me from complete despair. Still, if there were a chance....

I tried to shut it all out of my mind in the ensuing weeks. Daily life was ugly enough. Art ate his meals in his trailer. Mom and I spent most of our time in the house, avoiding him as much as possible.

Escrow closed on the little house just as the seasons shifted into spring. It was time to pack up and move out, but we hadn't gone to court yet, and I couldn't imagine simply leaving Ruf behind. We'd been inseparable for a year and a half. His constant affection and devotion had kept me from checking out early on life. He had saved me from a threatened abduction. His love was the only unconditional love I'd known in my life. How could I leave him behind?

Once again, I had no choice, no control over the circumstances of my life. Art hovered like a vulture over prey, watching our every move as we loaded our sparse belongings into a rental truck. Mom had sold nearly all her own things when she moved in with him. As we drove out of the yard, I was sick with grief, a dead weight sitting in my chest where my heart should be. And the day wasn't over. I had to return for the horses. When I rode out of the yard on my mare, leading my sister's horse, Art chained Rufus to the big pepper tree so he couldn't follow. I can still hear him barking....

At long last, I was safe from the specter of Art, but I found no joy and nothing to celebrate in our new situation. Without Ruf, I was simply bereft. The move did not mean changing schools, only bus stops, and again I found myself waiting for the bus each morning, the outsider who never spoke to the other students gathered there, my head lowered, my heart aching, this time without the company of my goofy dog to distract me.

Mom and I rarely spoke. She had her own loss to grieve, and so we avoided each other, walled off by our own pain. We were in limbo—waiting to go to court so that her divorce could be finalized, waiting for the tenants to vacate the house in Cypress so that we could return home and resume some semblance of the life we had before everything went so awry. I went to school each day, came home, sat in the front yard and played my guitar or listened to music for hours on end. On the weekends I took Topaz for long rides, but those were lonely journeys without Ruf.

School ended for the year and Peg came up. She had graduated high school and would stay with us now, moving back to Orange County in the fall to begin college. She sensed the sadness in the house, and she worked hard to lighten the mood, insisting that I take her shopping at the local swap meet or to church on Sundays, since she still didn't have a driver's license.

Not long after Peg arrived, Mom went out to do errands one day, returning hours later to tell us, "I got something for you. It's in the car." This was a familiar ruse; 'I got something for you but you'll have to unload the groceries to find it.' It was usually fresh strawberries, a pie, chocolate bars, or some other treat. Peg and I strolled out to the car, chatting casually. We found a puppy in the front seat.

He was a five-month-old, German Shorthaired Pointer. He had red, spotted fur, soft, floppy ears and a tail that never stopped wagging—well, the stump of a tail that had been docked. Mom had made friends during her short sojourn in Mira Loma. This dog's owners were breeders who had practically given him away because he didn't meet some sort of pedigree standard. Those who don't believe in love at first sight would have changed their minds to see my sister with that puppy that day.

She named him Jonah. He followed her everywhere. He was sweet and affectionate, so much like Rufus at that age that I could barely stand to be around him for fear that I would cry. After all we'd been through, I couldn't believe that Mom had brought home this dog. At the time, I didn't understand what she was trying to do. Having Jonah around—jumping up, begging me to throw a ball for him—only made the loss of Rufus worse. I sunk deeper into sadness.

Until one night in mid-summer.

When Mom and I had moved into the little house on Ridgeview Street, we'd met one of our neighbors, "Denny." He was a free-spirited twenty-one-year-old who had just moved back in with his father and step-mother while he was between jobs. One afternoon as I was playing my guitar, he walked up into the yard and introduced himself. He did odd jobs for us such as mowing the lawn and unloading hay. (Mom and I both had terrible hay fever and other allergies.) He would also come over just to hang out and talk, especially after Peg arrived. Evenings would find us sitting around outside (to avoid the oven-like heat of the poorly ventilated house), talking about music or books or philosophy.

One evening Denny came along for the ride as I headed for Mira Loma Market to pick up a few groceries. He had mentioned once that I 'seemed sad,' and I had told him a little about what had transpired in my life over the past two years. I don't know what it was that night—maybe going by the market or our conversation—but he urged me to drive by Art's, to check on Rufus. I didn't think I could. I hadn't been back there since we'd moved out. I was afraid of seeing Ruf chained to that tree, afraid of what it would do to me mentally and emotionally. I didn't think I could cope with the pain. But Denny was a product of the rebellious, "anti-establishment" mood of the early '70's, and he made light of "jail-breaking" Rufus. Emboldened by his suggestion that this would be an opportunity to perform "a big F you" to the man I hated, I drove over to Art's and pulled up across the street.

It was late in the evening. The lights were off in the trailer, indicating that Art was in bed. Without a moon or streetlights, I really couldn't see into the yard. I asked Denny to wait in the car, and I walked quietly across the street to the corner of the chain link fence. Into the still night air I uttered one syllable as loud as I dare whisper.

"Ruf!"

I heard a chain rattle and my heart sank—then soared as I saw a streak of white headed straight for me. The noise I heard had been his choke chain and tags. He bounded over the fence and jumped up again and again as I hugged him and kissed the top of his dirty head.

When I opened the car door, he jumped in, tail wagging, and we simply drove away.

Peg greeted Ruf joyfully when we arrived home, but Mom was unhappy with what I'd done and thought that it might jeopardize our chances of getting "full custody" of Rufus when we finally went to court. I muttered something glibly about possession being nine tenths of the law (even though I had no idea what that meant) and then ignored her.

Ruf got on famously with Jonah, and the two wore us out every day, playing and chasing balls. Although Mom was struggling to make ends meet on her small retirement income, she brought home treats and chew toys for both dogs on a regular basis.

That summer, for the first time in a very long time, I felt genuinely happy. With Rufus back by my side, I took long rides down along the Santa Ana River bottom or drove into Riverside to walk along the mall, sometimes bringing Jonah as well. Peg had taken a job as a waitress at a nearby golf course, and I often picked her up from work with both dogs in the car. And I was counting the days now before we'd move back to Orange County where I would reunite with my friends and begin my last year of high school. I couldn't wait.

Then one day I came home to find Ruf missing. I'd been gone all day, perhaps on a trip to the beach with friends, and when I returned, he was gone. Mom recounted some story about Art driving up in his truck, calling out to Ruf, and the dog running to jump in. I knew there was more to it than that. She had promised me she wouldn't tell him where we lived. When I questioned her she told me that Art planned to keep Rufus chained up until we went to court. How did she know? I would learn much later that she had continued to keep in touch with him after we moved out and eventually told him where we lived—after he promised not to take Rufus back.

That same week, Peg and I were sitting in the front yard with Jonah when he suddenly took off after the neighbor's cat, running straight into the street and into the path of an on-coming pick-up truck. He was still alive, but barely, when I lifted him gently and placed him in the front seat of Mom's car, hoping to get him to the vet's in time to save him. By the time I'd started the engine, he was gone. My sister sobbed with grief as I woodenly dug a grave in the backyard. The thought continued to course through my brain that at least Ruf was still alive somewhere.

Several days later, my beautiful, spirited mare was hit by a car and killed. We were never able to determine how she got out. Somehow, Mom's horse was still in the corral. We had a post and wire fence with a "hot wire" that kept the horses from leaning on it. When I went out to check on the horses late one night, the hot wire was lying on the ground, as if someone had placed it carefully there, and the corral gate was slightly open. I followed the path I thought Topaz might have taken, thinking I'd find her nibbling weeds in the dark and lead her back home. Eventually, I came to a major street where I saw the flashing lights of a patrol car. I told the officer I was looking for my horse.

"See that blood?" he said, using his flashlight to point to a large pool of blood in the road. "That's your horse's blood."

We moved back to Cypress at the end of August. I did not eat or sleep much and had dark circles under my eyes. My long hair fell out in handfuls when I washed it. I was deep in a depression that nothing could pull me out of. I don't remember moving back into our home or registering for school at John F. Kennedy High School. My friends had moved on, formed other social networks, but I didn't care. I spent most of my time alone. Mom went back to work and soon afterward bought me my own car, an older Volkswagen bug. After school I would drive to the beach and walk for hours. Sometimes I would stay up all night, then head to the beach to walk as the sun came up.

In those long walks, I imagined having Ruf with me to run along the water and chase toys out into the waves. That tiny ray of hope was what kept me going, putting one foot in front of the other, biding my time until our court date came up.

Finally, in January, it did.

I've never forgotten that day, standing outside the beautiful old courthouse in downtown Riverside, the magnolia blossoms scenting the air. I became acutely aware of my surroundings as I slowly trudged up the huge stone steps, dreading what the judge would say.

I had spoken to some friends in Riverside to let them know I'd be in town for the day, and one of them suggested I write a letter to the judge so I could give my side of the story. I still have the original copy, neatly typed on translucent "onion skin" paper. It reads:

Your Honor:

My mother will come before you today to obtain a divorce from my step-father.

Since I am only 16, I know I should not interfere with this case, but this case is interfering with me. Not the divorce itself, but the question about ownership of a dog named "Rufus." I believe <u>by law</u> he would be considered the property of my step-father, because Rufus was given to my step-father when he bought the property that would be the home of my mother and I when she married my step-father a few weeks later. I don't believe my step-father wanted Rufus, who was then just a pup, but my mother was probably the reason for my step-father keeping him.

I could not begin to relate all of the experiences and adventures Rufus and I shared in the nearly two years we spent together at my step-father's home. He loved me, he trusted me, and he protected me; my parents both worked and were gone from 6:30a.m. to 6:30p.m. during the week, and I was left alone except for the dog. The only time we were separated was while I was at school, and even then he accompanied me to the bus stop. I was very lonely when my mother remarried and we moved so far from all of my friends. Rufus was my constant companion, and we shared a love that was more like brother toward brother.

The dictionary defines "owner" as "one who has possession of," but I am of the opinion that a good dog cannot be possessed—he will stay with the person who gives him a "good home." By giving him a good home, I mean feeding, loving and caring for him. In the near two years that my mother and step-father lived together, it was I who did those things for Rufus.

I know I have been very frank in this letter, but I wanted you to realize the complete circumstances. My step-father will not allow me to have Rufus, though he knows the dog would be happier with me, and even goes to the extent of keeping him chained up so he cannot go in search of me. I have written this letter with the hope that you would understand, contemplate, and consider the emotional facts of this question of ownership. I put my trust now in you to give a just answer to the question of whether I'll be reunited with Rufus or not. Thank you for your valuable time.

Yours sincerely,

S. K. Murphy

Once inside the courthouse, Art greeted my mother politely, which only fueled my anger toward him. When our case was called, I sat in agony, my stomach turning, my heart pounding. I had given the letter to my mother who had promised to give it to her attorney to give to the judge. I could only hope that my words made a difference.

I hadn't realized until that moment in court, when the judge began his preliminary remarks, that my mother and step-father had only come to court for one reason. They had been married just over a year. They owned no property together, had no children together, and had easily sorted out their own belongings to make two separate households again. The judge asked them about this, "for the purposes of clarification," and they both agreed that they'd separated amicably.

"So," he continued, "you're both here because the only issue you can't agree on is the ownership of this dog—What's his name?" The judge paused and I watched him sift through some papers in front of him. "Rufus?" My mother and Art both nodded. Each was then given the chance to speak. My mother, in her usual direct, business-like manner, provided the background regarding how Rufus had come with the property but that the property was purchased with the intention of providing a home for us as a family. Without any sign of emotion, she told the judge quietly that I had cared for Ruf since he'd been a puppy, and that we were inseparable. Art, of course, lied. He spun long tales describing his attachment to the dog, proclaiming, "I'm the one that named him!" several times, telling the judge that he needed Rufus as a watch dog to "guard the livestock on the ranch" and that was why he'd kept him in the first place.

Finally, the judge asked me if I had anything to say. I considered replying that I had said it all in the letter I'd written, but that sounded disrespectful when I rehearsed it in my head.

"If you ask the dog, your honor," I finally answered, "he'll say he wants to come with me." Immediately I felt like an idiot for saying it, and my face flushed with embarrassment. But it was the truth, and somehow in the back of my mind I played out a scenario in which the judge would order Art to bring Rufus to the courthouse to let him choose for himself. Alas, these are the plots of Hollywood films, not the stuff of real life.

"I'm sorry," the judge began, "but the law states...." I heard nothing beyond those words, other than a door closing in my heart, the hard, cold metal of the latch clicking into place.

I have only one other brief memory from that day. Back outside, after we'd been told that dogs were "property," and that Rufus was therefore the "property" of Art, my mother stood talking to her attorney about the final details of the divorce. Just before we left, he pulled an envelope out of his pocket and handed it to her. "I thought you might want to keep this," he said. It was my letter. Unopened. He had never given it to the judge, and he offered no explanation for not doing so.

I had no idea I'd kept that letter until about a year ago when I was going through some boxes, deciding what to put in storage in advance of an upcoming move. I came across some memorabilia from high school, and I sat down in the basement to sift through it and reminisce. I lifted the small white envelope, the words "Important: Please read" handwritten across the front, from a box of old letters and keepsakes.

There are moments in which, unsuspecting, we come across pieces of our past, artifacts which contain such potent meaning, they can shake us to our core. Such was the case with this letter. I had no idea what was in the envelope until I carefully peeled it open, pulled out the yellowed pages and began to read. I spent the next several minutes sobbing. At that time, I had been pondering about what my next writing project should be, and I had considered writing about my beloved dogs. Finding that letter—as painful as it was to recall its content and all the memories behind it—constituted a sign to me that honoring Rufus by telling his story would be a very worthy use of my time.

I never saw him again after Art picked him up that day. I heard from neighbors that Art kept him chained up for a long time, and I didn't want to give him reason to continue doing so. When he was satisfied that I would not make the journey from Orange County to Mira Loma to try to reclaim him, he finally let him off the chain and allowed him to roam freely again. I know this because my mother told me. She and Art made peace with each other and remained friends, even after Art remarried. She would often stop by to visit, especially after he was diagnosed with emphysema. At first, she tried to give me updates on how Ruf was faring after each visit. Finally, I told her in no kind terms that I didn't want to hear anything else about him. It was simply too painful. I reneged, of course, when Art finally passed away many years later. Mom had called to ask if I wanted to attend the funeral. ("Why? To dance on his grave?" was my exact reply.) When I asked about Ruf, she said, "Oh, honey, he passed away years ago." I ended the conversation quickly, telling her to spare me the details.

When I was a young child, our family used to watch television dramas like Lassie and Rin Tin Tin. I loved to watch the dogs as they performed amazing feats, including understanding everything the humans said and often saving the lives of their owners. But I always assumed these behaviors were trained responses, tricks for the camera. If someone had told me then that a dog would one day put himself between me and a bad guy, that he would understand my need for protection and step in to ward off the danger, I would have laughed. With Rufus, I saw it with my own eyes, and it changed the way I thought of all dogs forever after. Before that incident, I knew that Ruf—for some unknown reason—just wanted to be with me. But I never would have imagined that a dog would be capable of this level of vigilance and comprehension. His assessment of the situation (and quick action) saved me, and after it happened I realized that he was always watching, not just me but the people around me as well. Like humans, dogs are able to observe and draw conclusions, and they do this far more often than we know.

We are just beginning to discover the amazing sensibility dogs have to chemical changes in the human body, which is why they're being trained in such duties as predicting on-coming seizures and detecting certain cancers. I honestly believe that Ruf picked me out and remained by my side when I came to live at Art's place, first because he detected my illness, his canine attributes compelling him to come to my aid, and later because he sensed my deep sadness. You may have had the experience yourself of a companion dog coming to you quite unexpectedly when you were sad or upset about something. I have no doubt that Ruf's response to me came from his innate canine character, a drive that most dogs have to defend, protect, and comfort. And this truth humbles me; Rufus picked me not because I fed him or cared for him, but because I was the needy one. In fact, as much as I tried to resist his attention in the beginning, he remained stalwart, unflinching in his quest to offer solace despite my ugliness toward him. This is why the wisest of men have characterized dogs as being noble. My Ruf—may he run forever free in those pastures just beyond the rainbow bridge—was the epitome of that characterization.

I have a photo of myself, Ruf and Topaz that was taken by a high school classmate. In the picture, I'm sitting cross-legged on someone's lawn, holding Topaz's reins as she nibbles at the grass. Ruf is by my side, my free arm slung casually across his back. This is the memory of him I will hold always, close to my heart.

Sapo

CHAPTER FIVE

In those days, demands were far less rigorous in terms of high school course work, and I had enough credits to graduate by the end of first semester of my senior year, just two weeks after we went to court regarding Rufus.

At the beginning of the year, I'd been excited about the prospect of getting out of school ahead of my class; from Kindergarten to my twelfth grade year, I never liked school, was never engaged in learning. I had little patience for high school games and cliques, and I looked forward to escaping an institution that only seemed to contribute to my dreary days.

Once I had my diploma, though, I didn't know what to do with myself. I tried getting a job, but I was only seventeen. Most places where I inquired wouldn't even let me fill out an application.

I began heading to the beach nearly every day. Often, I would just sit in my car and write—poems, journal entries, random thoughts... and letters.

Denny and I had stayed in touch after Mom, Peg and I moved back to Cypress. We wrote letters and sometimes talked on the phone. He had a quirky sense of humor and sometimes actually got me to laugh when I felt like I was walking in darkness, and he was the first person to come along in my life with whom I could discuss politics, particularly our government's involvement in the Vietnam war. We also spent a great deal of time talking about religion and spirituality. In my last months in Mira Loma, I had begun to occasionally attend a Sunday night gathering of "born-again" Christians—mostly to listen to the Christian rock bands. Denny was an atheist, and he had attended with me a time or two, for the avowed purpose of showing me how foolish I was to believe in such nonsense. We would have long spirited discussions over the phone about belief in God, and while I never agreed with his existential philosophy, I appreciated his courage to stand up for what he believed.

When we'd gone to court over Ruf, I'd called to let him know the outcome. He was outraged and went on a rant about the injustice of "the system." That was one time I did agree with him.

Occasionally Denny would make the drive down to Cypress, and we would head off in my little bug, down to the beach mostly, to spend the day sitting in the sand and talking about life. He understood how lonely I was. He asked me one day if I thought I'd ever get another dog, and I told him I just couldn't bring myself to consider it. I'd felt numb after losing Ruf, Jonah and Topaz in such a short time span, as if my heart were in shock. I was afraid to try to love another dog, afraid of another devastating loss.

I should have been suspicious the day Denny called and said he was coming down to see me and bringing someone he wanted me to meet. I thought it would be one of his friends from high school he used to talk so much about. When he pulled up in front of the house, I didn't see anyone in the car with him—until he opened the door, and a dog jumped out.

She was beautiful.

A cross between a German Shepherd and a Sheltie, she had the low-slung body of a Shepherd but the long hair and markings of a Sheltie. Her fur was mostly brown with lighter and darker tones, and she had a white blaze that went straight up the middle of her nose.

I called her, and she ran to me immediately. I knelt on the lawn to pet her and she curled into my open arms, licking my face and wagging her tail wildly.

"Do you like her?" Denny asked, laughing.

He had brought her down—"on loan"—from a rescue group in Riverside. Her "foster mom" had said that they suspected she had been abused; under certain conditions, she would become timid and fearful. She didn't seem that way now, as she ran around the yard sniffing and wagging her tail. He said that she could spend the day with us, and, if I wanted to keep her, she could stay. If I needed more time to think about it, he would simply take her back to the foster home.

She was soft and sweet and affectionate. How could I not like her? But part of me was holding back, and my response to her was reserved, as I had been with Jonah. I didn't want to love another dog I would lose.

We took her inside to see how she would react to the house and to other family members. When she had investigated every corner of every room, she jumped up next to me on the couch and leaned her body into mine. This would become a most familiar posture.

My mother thought she was beautiful. My sister loved her immediately. My own heart did not melt toward her, but I couldn't bear to disappoint Denny, so I told him that yes, I wanted to keep her. My heart still belonged to Rufus, but at least I would have someone to keep me company.

I wanted to name her "Tomodachi," the Japanese word for "friend," using "Tomi" as a nickname. A friend from school, Joyce Hatanaka, lived nearby, and I had great respect for her family and Japanese ancestry. Denny suggested I name her "Sapo," which means "toad" in Spanish. "But she's beautiful," I protested. "She deserves a beautiful name." The more names I suggested—"Celeste," "Angelique"—the more he pressed me to name her Sapo, reiterating how great the irony was and how funny it would be every time someone asked her name. It seemed he had already decided for me. Sad to say, I did what most young and naïve girls do when they're intimidated by an older, dominant male. I caved.

And so her name was Sapo—"Sapo D. Dog" as her full name. She deserved so much better, and I never stopped regretting my acquiescence. But as Shakespeare wisely said, "What's in a name? A rose by any other name would smell as sweet." And she was definitely a sweetheart.

For our first outing together, I took her to the beach. Denny had said she seemed to enjoy the drive down in his car, and when it came time to ride with me, she jumped into the front seat of my bug and sat down, eager to see where the trip might take her. She walked nicely on the leash—something Ruf would never do—and seemed happy to go wherever I led her, along the boardwalk, down the pier or into the sand.

The day was bittersweet. I had always imagined making this trip with Rufus, but I realized how different it would have been than my fantasy of it. In rural Mira Loma, with its country lanes and no sidewalks, Ruf would run ahead and circle back constantly as I rode Topaz, unfettered and free to explore where he would. In the heavily populated, ocean front community of Seal Beach, he would have always been leashed, restrained. The same would have been true at home in Cypress. Our walks would have been quite different than what he was used to, I would never have been able to take him out riding with me along the busy streets, and our "backyard" was mostly made up of a barn and horse corrals, with no real yard at all. Don't get me wrong; I would have moved back to Mira Loma if it meant having Ruf back in my life. But I tried to comfort myself that at least he had two acres on which to roam free.

Sapo was more than happy to trot along by my side. At home and in the house, she would wait until I sat down, then find a comfy spot nearby and curl around to wait for our next adventure. Mom had always allowed animals in the house—even my brother's rats and snakes—and from the first night, Sapo slept on my bed, her long body sprawled beside mine.

With each day that passed, I became more and more attached to her, and while at first I felt that in some way I was being disloyal to Ruf, I had to finally accept that there was, in fact, room in my heart for another dog companion. And once I reached that point, Sapo became my heart.

She went everywhere with me, from quick rides to the store to long drives back to Riverside to visit friends or favorite places. On those trips, I took her to the downtown mall where I had taken Ruf so many times and found that she, too, was a great judge of character. With most people, she would wag her tail and graciously accept compliments along with gestures of affection. Occasionally, though, someone would approach and she would move in close to me, her hackles raised, her tail tucked in fear. She only reacted negatively toward certain men. I never discovered why, though I suspected there was some smell, some article of clothing that triggered her anxiety. When this happened, I would kneel beside her and wrap my arms around her. Sometimes I could feel her trembling, and I wondered what she was remembering, wishing I could help her forget.

Her ability to remember, in fact, turned out to be one of her many endearing qualities. She quickly developed a close friendship with my sister, and Peg would always talk to her in a particular goofy voice— something like that of Grover, from Sesame Street. When Peg moved into an apartment with her best friend, Nancy, so they could be closer to the college campus, we didn't see her very often, sometimes not nothing to do, I decided to get some lunch at a local fast food restaurant a mile or so from the house. Sapo jumped in the bug with me, and we took off, getting there and heading back in record time. Like most teens, I pushed the speed limit, powered on by the rock music blaring from the radio. But just as I turned onto our block, someone in a Cadillac backed out of a driveway in front of me. I slammed on the brakes and tried to swerve around him, but he had just flown out into the street, never looking for oncoming traffic, and it all happened so fast I hardly had time to react. My front fender hit his back wheel. His car was fine. The front fender of the bug was crunched in all the way to the tire. I didn't care about all that, or the fact that my bean and cheese burrito was now sitting in a lump on the floor of the front seat. When I'd hit the brakes, Sapo had been catapulted forward. I always made her sit in the back seat—just in case something like this ever happened. But the jolt of the impact when we hit made the passenger seat fly forward, and she ended up in the front seat, hitting the dashboard. I clipped on her leash and brought her out of the car to walk around and calm down, as she was trembling and anxious. The driver of the other car never came over to apologize or see if we were alright. I recognized him right away. We'd gone to high school together, and in his senior year, he was always high. Someone in his house had called the police, and the officer was very kind. "Did he back out in front of you?" was the first question he asked. And then he asked about my dog. "She OK?" He helped me pull the bumper off my tire and as soon as I could get out of there, I headed home, no longer hungry. Sapo was fine, just shaken up, but the experience reminded me that I had precious cargo aboard when she was in the car, and unlike me, she couldn't see what was about to happen. After that, I drove more slowly... more like an adult.

Slowly, in the months after getting my diploma, with my dog—*my* dog—by my side, I began to recover from all that had transpired in the previous two years. Sapo's constant presence and her unwavering devotion, so like Ruf's, was a comfort I never stopped being grateful for, and I had Denny to thank. His gift of this dog touched me deeply as a token of his affection because he had seen what he thought I needed, and he responded to that need. I was so broken in the months after losing Rufus, then Topaz, it was as if I had endured some life-threatening physical trauma from which I was trying to heal, and he had brought me this dog as one would bring a teddy bear to a small child for solace. In that same sense, I kept her close to me always.

I also had Denny to thank for being my only available friend. In moving back to Cypress, I had been separated from the friendships it had taken so long to establish in Riverside, and as I have said, upon my return, I had found that the friends I'd had prior to leaving had now formed other friendships. Graduating midterm didn't help, as it left me alone all day with nothing to do while most everyone I knew was still in school. The letters and phone calls I exchanged with Denny had changed in nature, moving from friendship to something more intimate, so when he suggested marriage, I agreed. He was not the type of man I had envisioned myself with years before when my naiveté had allowed me to imagine a future husband who was tall, dark, handsome and much like me in personality. Denny was a risk taker, at times a scofflaw, and he had issues with authority figures, especially law enforcement officers. He claimed to be liberal in his thinking, but in his unguarded moments, I saw a man who was judgmental and often scathingly critical toward others. Still, he had offered me tenderness during a time when no one else reached out to me. And all things considered, I had come to believe the things that Art had told me over and over, that I was worthless and unattractive. I thought it presumptuous to assume that if I rejected Denny's offer, another one from someone more compatible would be forthcoming. And he had promised to buy me a house. The thought of moving out, of having our own place with room for horses and dogs and the liberty to live life as we chose made me starry-eyed in anticipation. Childish, I know, but I was still a child at seventeen.

We married in June, a month before my eighteenth birthday, in a ceremony held on the front lawn of the same church whose Sunday evening services we now attended regularly. I wanted the wedding to take place outside, and having it so meant Sapo could be present. It was an informal affair, with most of our friends in jeans and bare feet in the soft spring grass. Sapo is there in the pictures along with my handful of friends from school and our family members.

Denny had taken a new job with his brother-in-law in the months prior to our wedding and almost immediately had begun saving up a down payment to buy a home. That quest to find just the right house is what led to dire consequences for my beautiful dog.

In the first weeks after our marriage, we lived with Denny's sister and brother-in-law, in the garage of their home which had been converted into a large added on room. We did this to keep our rent low, as every spare penny was going into our down payment fund. As newlyweds, however, we were anxious to move into our new place, and so we spent a good part of every weekend meeting with realtors or out looking for property.

On a warm Saturday afternoon in July, we picked up a newspaper in Riverside and saw an ad describing what sounded like our dream home. We found a pay phone and called a realtor we'd been working with, and he agreed to meet us downtown to discuss the property. As always, we had Sapo with us. When "Dean" arrived in his sharp, clean Cadillac, he told us a bit about the home, then suggested we take a drive with him to go look at it. I suggested taking separate cars, since we had Sapo with us, but he insisted that the property was "a five-minute drive away," and that she would be fine waiting in the car for us. Denny, who had been excited by the property's description and eager to fulfill his promise that we would soon own a home, also assured me that leaving the dog in the car—with the windows open slightly—would be fine for the short period of time we'd be gone. With an uneasy feeling, I agreed.

The drive to the property did not take five minutes, it took fifteen. Before we were ever there, I began calculating how long it would take us to get back. I was about to tell Dean to turn around and take us back to my car, when he finally pulled up in front of a run-down house in a crime-ridden, unincorporated area outside the city limits. Denny could tell that I was upset as soon as we got out of the car, but he assumed it had to do with being disappointed in the property. I walked through the house as quickly as I could, told Dean it wasn't what we were looking for, and asked him to please take us back to my car. The conversation that had been so lively on the trip out had been quenched by my fretful demeanor, and very little dialog took place on the return journey. Along the way, I never stopped sending up silent prayers. Despite the fact that it was early evening, the temperature outside was extremely hot, and I knew the temperature in my little car would be well over one hundred degrees by the time we got back. I prayed my dog would still be alive when we returned.

I had the door of Dean's car open as he pulled up to the curb, and I stepped out the moment he stopped, leaving my husband to dismiss the man. I ran to my car and threw open the door. Sapo was not in the back seat. As I stood holding the door in confusion, I heard a scrabbling sound and saw movement. To this day, I don't know how she managed it, but she had somehow crawled under the front passenger seat, seeking an escape from the oppressive heat. She clawed and scrambled her way out of the car, and I sank to my knees on the sidewalk, my arms around her neck, my head bowed in abject apology. I have done some foolish things in my life. This stands as one of the most idiotic. That I allowed two adult men to convince me that my dog would be fine left alone in a car on a hot day is something I've never forgiven myself for, and I hope I never do. It was a lesson that has lasted a lifetime, and I can only wonder what would have become of me if Sapo had not survived.

We did eventually find the perfect home. Ironically, it was in Mira Loma.

We had tried to find a place in Riverside, near Denny's job, but we quickly realized we couldn't afford the homes close to the city—not if we wanted horse property. So our search took us farther and farther outside the city limits until finally one day we found what we were looking for in Mira Loma. I had told my new husband that I had in mind a yellow house with a white picket fence. As we pulled onto Ridgeview Street—the street where we had met—we both saw the "For Sale" sign at the same time. The house was yellow with a white picket fence around the front yard. The property had a hay shed and horse corrals. We bought it for $19,000—a price my mother said was far too high for a three-bedroom home on a half acre of land.

And so we settled into married life. In the first months, I spent the weekdays working on fixing up the house after Denny went to work. But in the fourth month of our marriage, I became pregnant. Our first child, a daughter, was born on my nineteenth birthday.

I remember bringing her home from the hospital and showing her to our other daughter—Sapo—who sniffed the blanket, nuzzled the sleeping creature tucked in there, and wagged her tail in delight. We were a family.

Those first years were nearly idyllic for me.

I loved being a stay-at-home mom. I would rise early to have breakfast with my husband and see him off to work, then settle in to read or write until Shalome— "Shali"—woke up. In awe of the miracle that she was, I spent hours just holding her, watching her, attempting to catch every new thing she learned or saw or tasted or touched. When she was old enough to sit up in a baby back pack, we would go for long walks around the neighborhood, Sapo joining us, of course. Sapo was the perfect family dog, always gentle, always tolerant. And there was quite a bit she had to tolerate.

While reading the classified section of our local paper one day, I saw an ad which offered a "free gray goose" to a loving home. This young goose had been at the bottom of the pecking order and the other geese in his gaggle were constantly picking on him. The owners loved him and wanted a safe home for him. By this time we had a large garden going and I'd read that geese were organic machines as they ate the bugs off the plants while simultaneously fertilizing the soil. We brought our goose home, named him "Fred" after a good friend, and gave him the run of the backyard. Sapo was great and never chased him, which was probably wise; once he'd established his domain, visitors to the yard had to be accompanied by a family member. Geese make excellent guard animals, and Fred would always let us know when someone came around. One afternoon I heard a commotion in the back yard and looked out to see two very large men—friends of ours—with their backs against the shed wall, wielding gardening tools. My husband had told them to help themselves when they'd ask to borrow our small tractor, but hadn't warned them about Fred. They didn't want to bother me, so rather than knock on the door, they just headed out back. Fred had backed them against the wall, hissing and honking, and they looked to be in fear for their very lives before I calmly walked out and waved my gallant goose away.

Often in the afternoons when Shali was old enough to play outside I would sit on the patio and play my guitar while she played with her dolls. For some reason, Fred was fascinated by the music and singing. He always came up from the garden to be my audience of one, standing just inches away, listening intently.

Other animals found sanctuary with us as well.

On a hot summer afternoon while Shali and I were cooling off with the sprinkler in the front yard, a mysterious guest walked in through the picket gate. He was a big brown dog with a large round head like a Mastiff—and deep brown eyes with heavy brows that gave his face a pensive look. He ambled in and came slowly up the walk, head down and tail tucked, looking for all the world like a hobo with his hat in his hand. When I spoke to him, he lifted his head slightly. His tail swung slowly back and forth.

I made Shali stay back from him until I had inter- acted with him enough to determine that he was gen- tle and friendly. Docile would be a better term. He introduced himself amiably to Sapo, allowed us to lav- ish him with caresses and questions ("Whose dog are you?" "Are you hungry?"), then curled up on the grass to watch us play. He was wearing a collar but no tags, and he looked well cared for.

When Denny came home I explained how our guest had arrived. He shrugged and went inside to shower. I didn't know what else to do, so Shali and I went inside as well. The next morning, we found the big brown dog curled up in a ball sleeping by the front door. I invited him in for some breakfast, and he ate side by side with Sapo. Denny went off to work, and I set about the daily tasks of dishes and laundry and raising a child. The big brown dog found a sun spot on the old linoleum floor in the kitchen, curled up and sighed deeply. From time to time as I went about my house- hold duties, I would stop for a moment and stroke his head. After awhile, I started calling him Jedediah, a name I referenced with strength and wisdom. By the time Denny arrived home from work that day, it had already been shortened to Jed-Dog.

The only way to describe Jed is to simply say he was an old soul. He had come to us—but his decision to do so clearly wasn't based on need. He ate the food we gave him slowly and politely, grateful for it but not frantic to wolf it down. He did not fawn over us or beg for affection. He appeared content to find a safe, out-of-the-way spot, lie down and quietly observe the goings on of the household. At night, he would curl up beside Sapo on our bedroom floor. I heard his long, deep sighs as I drifted off to sleep.

One evening two weeks after Jed appeared, Denny and I, having put Shali to bed, were sitting in the front yard with the dogs, trying to escape the heat of the house. A pick-up truck pulled up and a young man got out. As he walked through our front gate, Jed uncurled himself and ambled toward him.

"Don't worry," I called to the stranger, "he's friendly."

"I know," the young man said, "he's my dog."

He went on to tell us that Jed—"Harley"—had disappeared from his yard two weeks before, and he'd been looking for him ever since.

"I just live down the street," he said, "on the corner across from the convenience store." We knew the house well. It was a "party house," with drugs, loud rock music and constant traffic going on day and night.

We introduced ourselves and offered him a chair. The young man's name was John. When he sat down, Jed leaned against him, tilting his big head back to look up into his master's eyes.

"I don't understand why he left," John said. "I've had him since he was a pup, and I nursed him through distemper." Jed was neutered and Sapo was spayed, so we knew it had not been the lure of her estrus that brought him to the yard.

I went inside and returned with a glass of iced tea for John. We sat talking for awhile about the dogs, about the neighborhood. We assured him that Jed-Dog had come to us by his own free will, and we'd never made an effort to keep him; he just had not wanted to leave. Without tags, we had no way to search for his owner. John shook his head. Finally, he said, "It's peaceful here. Quiet. It isn't like that where I stay." He paused, then went on. "I don't think I was giving him enough attention." We saw him brush tears from his cheek, and my heart ached for him. A picture was becoming clear; Jed had felt unwanted in the chaos of that environment, especially after John had begun to neglect him. When he came to us, he'd been looking for the comfort of human companionship.

"We love him," I said. "You can always leave him with us if you're not able to take care of him. You could always come by and visit."

"No," he said, shaking his head again, "I need to do right by him. I love this dog. He's been with me through all kinds of shit." He wrapped his arms around the dog's neck, laying his cheek atop Jed's big head, and I found it impossible to fight back my own tears.

John stood and thanked us. When he shook my husband's hand, his face reflected a new resolve. We knew that the well-being of his dog would now become a priority in his life. We told Jed good-by and watched him follow John to the truck and hop in. We never saw either one of them again, not even a glimpse of John's truck in the neighborhood, and we hoped it was because John had made some changes in his life, found a place more quiet and conducive to the contentment of a well-deserving dog.

And then came Luke. Jed-Dog had appeared in the summer. The following autumn, I walked out to get the mail one very foggy morning from our rural box. Curled up in the dirt next to the road I saw what I thought was a dead dog. I assumed he'd been hit by a car. There were leash laws in San Bernardino County back then, but they were never enforced. Most property owners in Mira Loma had insecure fences, and in the 1970's, most of our neighbors considered spaying and neutering a luxury to be afforded only by the affluent of the community, so the sight of unaltered dogs roaming the neighborhoods was common. Speed limits were also ignored. Sadly, road kill was also a common sight, as cats, dogs, opossums, chickens and goats often strayed onto the narrow country roads.

When I approached the dog in the dirt, he lifted his head. I spoke to him, and he stood up, shook off some of the dirt and drizzle that had accumulated on his fur, and looked at me with pale blue eyes. He was an Australian Shepherd, mostly white with some gray patches that were so light they looked blue. He was trembling, whether from the cold or fear, I couldn't tell. He had no collar.

"Whose dog are you?" I asked, kneeling down. He came to me, wagging his tail, and leaned against my leg as I petted him. I took him in, dried him off, fed him, and by the end of the day he was responding to the name I had picked out for him—Luke.

Like Jed, Luke appeared to be housebroken, and like Jed, he was well-mannered and unobtrusive in the household. He and Sapo got along fine, Shali loved having yet another dog to play with, and I enjoyed his company. While Jed had been content to simply curl up somewhere, Luke, like Sapo, would follow me around the house or the yard, curious to see what the next task entailed.

As I had with Jed, I called the county dog pound and reported finding a male Australian Shepherd in Mira Loma, and I was told, as I had been before, to "bring the dog in" if I didn't want to care for it. I knew that meant a death sentence; Luke would be euthanized in seventy-two hours if no one claimed him. So we simply kept him safe and waited. No one came for him.

And then one day, as mysteriously as he had appeared, Luke was gone. I let him out into the backyard with Sapo one morning, and when I opened the door to let the dogs in, she was there alone. We never saw him again.

I wondered about the transience of such dogs, and I know now that it has to do with canine nature. As "dog whisperer" Cesar Milan has taught us, dogs are essentially pack animals, and as such, they seek a pack leader. In the absence of one, they become anxious and restless. And, I would add to that, lonely. Looking back over my own experience with dogs, I can see that this was the case with Jed and Luke. While I never did discover who Luke's people were, I suspect they had neglected to spend quality time with him, and eventually he, like Jed, went in search of companionship.

Had I only known this experience with Jed and John was a harbinger of things to come in my own life, I would have tried to be more receptive, to learn the lesson of this canine drama that had been presented before my eyes. But as I have said, I am a slow learner....

CHAPTER SIX

When Shali was four, my husband and I brought home our second child, a boy. Before we married, Denny had claimed repeatedly that his intention after marriage was to have one biological child, then adopt "five or six" more, and I had indicated just as often that I didn't really care for little kids, and that I intended to invest my time in establishing myself as a writer rather than procreating.

But I had loved having Shali. In fact, I had so immersed myself in the study of pregnancy and childbirth that after she was born, I began teaching childbirth preparation classes. And raising her had been an unexpected joy. In truth, we were children together, baking bread, making poppy seed cake for Daddy, playing with the animals or reading picture books for hours. I began to consider that another child might be twice the fun, and my husband's rationale—now that I had come to love the role of "Mama"—made sense to me. As part of his desire to revolutionize society, he felt that producing more children was simply adding to the global challenge of over-population. His parents had been successful foster parents, and he understood how many children languished in foster care while awaiting a permanent family. For some, the stability and security of a permanent home never came.

We had not set out to adopt an infant, but since our son was bi-racial, he was considered a "special needs" case. In fact, the adoption agency we went through had no other approved parents who would consider adopting him.

Ezra was named after children's author and illustrator Ezra Jack Keats. He was a different baby than Shali had been. Where she had been content to gaze out at the world in wonder (as long as someone was holding her), he was an irritable, fussy baby, stubborn and demanding from an early age. And while Sapo was happy to welcome a new sweet-smelling bundle, Shali's jealousy was acted out in tantrums and defiance. As Ezra grew from infant to toddler, however, she came to adore her little brother—so much so that she decided more siblings could only make for more fun. We would eventually add another daughter, Joanna, and another son, Sam. Shali was right; with the addition of each child the house became noisier... but much more entertaining.

In 1978, I had begun writing my first book. My childbirth classes were going well, but students often complained about the highly clinical nature of the books in my lending library. "You're a writer," one couple told me. "Can't you write a book about this stuff that's easier for us to understand?" I sent out a book proposal and was under contract with a national publisher before the book was even written.

To get things done, I would often rise at 4:00a.m. and work on the book for two hours before the kids woke at 6:00. When they took naps in the afternoon, I would edit and revise what I'd written in the morning. It took me less than a year to finish the book, and I submitted the manuscript a month ahead of schedule.

In that same year, Denny became the pastor of a small nondenominational church.

I suppose I should backtrack a bit.

Although I married an atheist existentialist, in the weeks after we married and returned to Riverside, Denny and I became regulars at that same Sunday evening service I used to attend only occasionally. He had told me he intended to keep going until he had "shot down" every argument I had for a belief in the spiritual world. But what transpired was his own conversion experience and a sudden about-face. In one night, he went from atheist to religious zealot. "I hope you know," he warned me, "I will not be content to simply live a Christian life. I have to preach the gospel, and I want to have my own church some day."

Frankly, I never believed that would happen, and I assumed that as quickly as he had reversed himself in his disdain for all things related to Christianity, he would work through his new passion for divinity and find some other aspect of life to throw himself into.

But as time went on, we attended church more and more frequently, and he went from deacon to elder to finally being offered the position of pastor for a tiny new church which had just formed in nearby Chino. Months before, we had put our house on the market at the top of the 1970's housing bubble. The property we had purchased for $19,000 in 1972 had just sold in 1978 for $50,000, and we had big plans to move to Northern California and raise our children away from the smog and overpopulation of the Inland Empire. Early in our marriage, after Denny discovered that, with the exception of a long, hot family road trip when I was nine, I had never been out of Southern California, he took me on a trip up the coast, acting as my tour guide in beautiful places like Morro Bay, San Simeon and Monterey. I fell in love with the green rolling hills dotted with ancient oak trees in Central and Northern California, and he promised me we would relocate there as soon as he could arrange it. We had listed our home for the sole purpose of finally making the move.

Then one night as we entertained a couple from our church for dinner, my husband dropped a bombshell. Escrow would close on our property in one week, and I had already happily begun packing. When asked what our plans were, my husband responded that he'd been offered a position as pastor of the church in Chino, and that God had told him he was to stay in the area and take the position. Before that moment, he had never mentioned his intent to me.

My heart was broken in an instant—in front of our company.

But I can't say that I was surprised by the unilateral decision he had made.

He had long ago left behind his sense of partnership in our marriage. The more deeply he became immersed in the tenets of fundamental Christianity, the wider the gap had grown between us. Now I was the one challenging the conservative values he suddenly began to espouse—that wives were subject to their husbands, that divorce—for any reason—was a sin, and that God called only males to the ministry. (Thus, when a song leader was needed for the new church, I could not apply for the position, despite the fact that I was now the pastor's wife and had been playing my guitar and singing in church for years.) The few female pastors who existed at the time were not following God's plan, according to my husband, and were also highly suspect as being "lesbians." His condemnation for homosexuals was overt, which led to some long and heated conversations concerning friends I'd made—in the church—who happened to be gay.

I had secretly hoped that in the move out of Southern California and away from the strict fundamentalism of what was quickly becoming the most popular church in the Inland Empire (Harvest Christian Fellowship), my husband and I would have a new start. I wanted to believe that the basic foundation of our friendship remained, and that striking out on a new life together in a beautiful place, where we initially would have only each other and our children, would stitch us back together.

Even with his announcement that we would be staying in the area—and that I would soon be a pastor's wife, something I would never have signed on for—I didn't want to accept that our marriage was irreparable. Sadly, the unraveling had begun long ago, and it would only get worse.

The most pressing issue at that moment was finding a place to live. Since our home in Mira Loma would close escrow any day, we needed to find another house. On the night that Denny had told our company about his plans, I found myself sliding into such a deep sadness that I couldn't speak to him about any of it. The next day I told him that since he'd begun making all the decisions for us, he could find a place for us to live, that I wasn't interested in being involved in looking, which was the truth. When he replied that he had taken the day off work to go house-hunting in Chino, I finally understood why he hadn't said anything before; his plan had been to use the money from the sale of our home to buy something close to his new church. Property values were higher there, as it was a more affluent area (at least where he had devised to move us), so he would use all the equity we'd earned for a down payment on a new place.

But with prices for new homes being what they were, we couldn't afford a home in Chino. And so we moved to Fontana.

In the 1970's, Fontana was notorious for three things: Drugs, gangs, and an active chapter of the Ku Klux Klan that still organized public parades and demonstrations. When my husband told me he'd signed escrow papers on a property in that city, my first thought was to give up on the marriage and leave. But where would I go? I had two young children, no money of my own and no employment history, no friends outside of our church (and certainly no one in the church would support my leaving). I had no other option, so I made the move, but I told him clearly, "Nothing good can come of this."

Nothing did.

The house sat in the middle of a large property which was encircled with chain link fencing. We had neighbors only on our west side; on the east side was an abandoned olive orchard and beyond that were some industrial complexes. We were bordered on the north by Interstate 10 and the Southern Pacific rail-road.

The fencing on the property wasn't terribly secure, and I worried constantly about the horses getting out. I still had my Shetland pony, and someone from the church had given me a young mare to train.

One evening just before bedtime, I let Sapo out, but when I called her to come back in, she didn't return. When I expressed concern, Denny waved it off and headed for bed. "She'll come back," he muttered. It had become a familiar refrain as our dog's behavior in the previous year had begun to change.

The people who lived behind us in Mira Loma had raised pigs. On warm summer days when the wind blew in the afternoon, the strong odor of pig by-products often wafted over us. There came a day when Sapo was missing from the yard, and I fretted for hours, thinking someone had taken her somehow. In the late evening, we heard her tags jingle at the door, and as soon as we let her in, we knew where she'd been—she reeked of pig stench, and so did the house after she'd been inside for a few minutes. We hastily dragged her off to the tub and scrubbed it, but it was almost impossible to get the smell out of her fur and skin. Several days later, she was in the garden with me as I weeded, and I watched her go to the back fence and squirm under. I called her sharply. She looked back over her shoulder for a moment, and it was clear from her eyes that she was deciding. Then she was off, trotting through the weeds toward the neighbor's pig pens.

Then, I felt betrayed. Now, I understand. Dogs need fresh air, new scenery, exercise and adventure. I had become busy with child care, house care, church and teaching childbirth classes. Gone were the long walks and bike rides we'd taken when Shali was a baby. I expected Sapo to settle in, be content with my company, as Jedediah had been. But she was only seven, and she still had the need to get out and explore her world. When I didn't take her, she went out on her own.

I had convinced myself that the lure was simply the pig farm itself, so when we moved to Fontana, my thought was that, with the tall chain link fences, her roaming days were over. In truth, I'm sure that the now constant tension in the house got to her as much as it got to me, and her own anxiety level had grown. Once we moved in, unhappy as I was to be there, I never took her—or the kids—for a single walk around the neighborhood. Sapo had begun to explore on her own.

Denny was right, that first time; she did finally come home, but it wasn't until the early morning hours, just before the sun came up. She'd never been out all night before. When I heard the familiar jingle of her collar at the back door, I let her in, then sat on the kitchen floor with her, my arms around her neck, tears in my eyes. If only I had understood what she really needed.

That day, I found where she'd been getting out, and I asked my husband to fix the fence. He told me he would when he had time, but that time never came. Days later, Sapo took off again. This time, she didn't return.

I let her out one evening just before we went to bed, then called her to come back in a few minutes later. When she didn't come, I went outside looking for her. I knew she'd gone out of the yard again, but I forced myself to believe that she'd be back home again when I woke up. She wasn't. I dressed quickly and walked the perimeter of the property at daybreak, calling her name, expanding my search to include the olive orchard next to us. Nothing. I returned to the house—the house I never wanted, in the city I never would have chosen to live in—laid my head on my arms at the kitchen table and wept.

Sapo's love was unconditional, her companionship constant, just as Ruf's had been, and if I needed anything in those bleak months and years as my marriage disintegrated, I needed unconditional love and affection. Sapo was my anchor, and without her, my life was set adrift once again.

I spent the first day calling the pound, placing a lost and found ad in the paper, praying and hoping.

The next morning found me back at the kitchen table, my head in my arms, despondent. Suddenly I heard her collar and tags. I jumped up and threw open the back door. There was nothing there. I was to experience this phenomenon a number of times in the weeks that followed. My husband carefully, condescendingly explained that I was imagining the sound, or hearing something else that my mind interpreted as that sound. But I know what I heard. In the quiet hours of the early morning, while the rest of the family slept, in the time that I usually spent writing or reading, drinking tea with Sapo at my feet, I would hear that distinctive sound, almost as if my mind were remembering and re-playing it.

I want to believe that some kind, dog-loving people found her and kept her without trying to find us, convincing themselves that her owners must not have cared for her. I don't want to think that she was hit by a car or attacked by coyotes or bitten by a rattlesnake while she wandered the rural roads and back lots of Fontana. I did spend hours driving around, my eyes searching, searching, but to no avail. It has been a life-long sadness never to know what happened to her.

She had only been gone a month or two when my husband brought home another dog. A woman at church had been looking for a home for a very sweet Doberman Pinscher, so Denny volunteered us as potential new owners. I understand what he was trying to do; Sapo had been a profound comfort to me after I'd lost Rufus, and this went a long way toward helping me heal from the emotional trauma surrounding those years. But simply bringing me a replacement dog before I'd fully given up hope of finding Sapo could not console me. We'd lost a family member, and his gesture this time, after all that had transpired between us in recent months, could only be interpreted as his desire that I move forward and 'get over it.' I resented him for that, and for finally repairing the chain link fence only after he'd brought "Mosie" home.

Unfortunately, fixing the fence and having a Doberman pinscher trotting around the yard wasn't enough to deter burglars.

A week after Mosie came to us, we arrived home from mid-week Bible study to discover that someone had broken into the house through the bathroom window. They'd made off with my typewriter and some stereo components. I was grateful to have had my guitar with me, as it is the only material possession I own—even today—that I would consider irreplaceable.

As I said, Mosie was a sweet dog, and she probably stood nearby and wagged the stump of her docked tail as the burglars went about the business of breaking into our home. To me, this was a testimony to the dog's amiable personality, which made me feel a bit better about keeping her; I'd been concerned about having her around the kids, since the breed has a reputation for being aggressive.

Angered by the break-in, however, my husband decided to enroll Mosie in "protection training." While I argued that subjecting a loveable dog to alleged "training" that would render her aggressive, Denny maintained that Mike, a member of our church with a guard dog training business, would teach Mosie to protect our property without compromising her good disposition. As with many aspects of our relationship and the running of our household, I was out-voted, two to one. (My husband always allowed himself two votes—his and God's.)

Against my wishes, Denny took Mosie to her first training class. What he described to me afterward I can only characterize as cruel and barbaric. Mike's approach was to first treat the dog with kindness and affection. When he had won her trust, he immediately betrayed it by inflicting some form of bodily harm, such as poking her in the ribs or yanking her ear until she yelped in pain. In this way, he said, he was teaching her to "trust no one." This kind of treatment of a dog incited far more anger in me than the burglary had. Despite my repeated requests that Denny stop the training, he continued to take Mosie, and I watched her personality change before my eyes. The young, energetic dog who loved everyone became an over-stressed, anxious animal that paced constantly. When she began to dig huge holes in the front yard, Denny sought Mike's advice.

"Fill the hole with water," he told my husband, "and hold her head under until she can't breathe." I watched in horror and disbelief from the window one day as he did exactly that. What kind of man had I married? He seemed suddenly very much like the step-father I had abhorred. I don't remember what it was I said to him—perhaps it was a threat to leave—but I made it clear that I would not tolerate any further acts of cruelty. It had already been determined that Mosie was a "wash-out" in terms of her protection training. Mike had come to our house in the night dressed in black and rattled the fences in a ridiculous mime of someone breaking in. Mosie had run to the fence, no doubt picked up Mike's scent, and simply waited to see what he would do, exhibiting no aggressive behavior. The men got together afterward, and I was later told that I had undermined the entire process, that as long as I insisted on "babying" her, Mosie would never become a guard dog. "Thank God," was my only response.

By the end of that ill-fated year in Fontana, Denny had found a place we could afford in Chino, so we moved again, but the chasm between us grew greater every day, and five years later, my husband and I divorced.

What transpired between us in the last five years of what had become a toxic union is the stuff better suited for tell-all books and slander sheets, and it is not my intention to wander off track here and recount the rage-filled days of my leaving. Suffice it to say, we did not part amicably.

In making the arrangements for the kids and I to move out, I found a loving home for Mosie with a patient couple who understood that she was a great dog who had been treated badly. Letting her go was difficult, but I had no choice; we'd be living in rental housing, and my husband had sworn he would give me not a single cent in child support if I left.

It is significant, I think, that I have no photographs of Mosie. The brief span of time in which she was with us marks a dark point in my life. I do, however, have many, many pictures of Sapo taken in the early years of my marriage. My favorite is one of myself, my daughter in 'feet' pajamas and our beloved dog sprawled on her back in the bed between us. It depicts a lazy weekend morning, the three of us snuggled into the covers for warmth, the love between us apparent on our faces.

Despite my husband's ill-fitting name for her, I will always think of my beautiful, sweet, teddy-bear of a dog as "Tomodachi," because she was such a friend to me. Like Ruf, she loved me unconditionally, and like Ruf, she deserved far more than she ever received in return. But I learned from her a lesson I have never forgotten, and that is this: Our dogs are like small children. They cannot always communicate what it is they need, and because of this, we need to be ever vigilant, attentive to the subtle signals they send to us. Above all, we need to see the world from their perspective, to understand their need for stimulation, the primal urge to explore new sights and smells and sounds on a regular if not daily basis. Put in perspective, it is very little that they ask of us in exchange for all that they give.

Alex

CHAPTER SEVEN

On a warm spring day, I ambled slowly through the indoor concrete and chain link kennels at the City of Upland animal shelter, my eyes moving over each confined dog, though I can't easily define what it was I sought. A connection? Kinship? The potential for abject devotion? Curled on the hard floor at the back of one enclosure was a large black mass of fur. When I knelt beside the kennel, sad brown eyes watched me. The dog did not lift his head from where it rested on his paws until I spoke to him. I said something in a quiet tone, and the dog unwrapped himself cautiously, stood, stretched and walked toward me, wagging his tail slowly. The behavior mimicked almost exactly the behavior of another dog I had seen in this same place nearly a year before, possibly even in this same kennel.

In the first year after Denny and I separated, I moved four times. Finally, with the divorce proceedings over with and the sale of our home in Chino finalized, I was able to find a house to rent in Chino Hills. I had been looking for months, but few landlords will rent to a single woman with four children, especially when she has no source of income. Understandably so. Denny had remained true to his word; he would never give me money or support in any way for the children he had so enthusiastically brought into our home. I knew him well enough to know how events would play out, and I understood that it would be up to me now to provide for my children. With this in mind, I enrolled in the local community college. I needed a breadwinner's salary and in order to obtain that, I needed an education beyond high school. My goal was to earn a bachelor's degree and teaching credential. Given my introverted personality, I never envisioned myself as a teacher. But teaching would afford me the greatest amount of time with my kids, including summers off, and so I simply chose that profession as best fitting my need. With student loans, some grant money from the state of California, food stamps and a modest cash allowance from the county in the form of Aid to Families with Dependent Children, we had enough income to subsist on. We were living at the poverty level, but I would manage to make ends meet.

The house in Chino Hills was perfect for us, with a large fenced backyard and an enclosed front courtyard lined with rose bushes. I could have chosen a place with much lower rent, but I was determined to raise my kids in a quiet, settled neighborhood offering room to roam and far from the dangers of more populated areas.

We moved in just before Christmas in 1984. The past year had taken its toll on all of us—separating, moving, trying to get settled with almost no financial reserves. But somehow we made it, and when we found ourselves in a stable situation without the constant tension of an imploding marriage, we realized we were happy... for the first time in a long time.

People often ask me how I did it. My pat answer is, "Without sleeping." Honestly, it was exhausting, but I would do it all again in a heartbeat. This was my daily routine:

Get the kids up early. Make lunches while they eat breakfast. Get everyone dressed and ready for school. Find Sam's shoes. (I swear not a morning went by that wouldn't find three-year-old Sam wandering the house, blankie in hand, bemoaning the loss of his shoes. He took them off in the weirdest places, and it was always left to me—in the midst of the usual morning chaos—to find them.) Load everyone plus books, backpacks, supplies and lunches into the car. Drive Shali, Jo and Ezra to their old neighborhood elementary school in Chino (because I'd promised they could finish the school year there) and drop them off. Drive to a preschool just south of Chino and drop Sam off. Get back in the car and brush away the tears of guilt for not staying home with this last baby, then head to the campus to attend classes all day. In the afternoon, pick up Sam first, then the others at school, then head home. Supervise homework while making dinner. Supervise the rotation of baths and showers while doing the dishes. Put all four to bed while refereeing any residual fights or squabbles. And then... finally... crack open the books to complete math homework, read literature or study for tests.

I could only fully attend to my homework after the kids were asleep. More than once in those days, I fell asleep on the livingroom floor trying to work through algebra problems.

Somehow though, despite the frenetic energy required to maintain it, we made it all work. And I loved college. I loved my literature classes and Psychology, and I even loved the challenge of solving quadratic equations. I surprised myself at the end of the first semester by getting straight A's. Doing so made me determined to do it again in second semester, and I did. And suddenly the first year was completed and it was summer and we had time again, time to play or dance to the cool '80's music we loved or ride bikes or take walks down to the creek to search for crawdads. Once a week we took a trip to the library in Chino. We would return home loaded down with books, and the kids would spend hours in the afternoons reading. We were poor, but life was good, and I knew the poverty was only temporary. My kids were safe and happy, far removed now from all the negative energy that had at one time colored every day of our lives. I could not have asked for more.

Of course, I was a young single woman, and, well, I didn't want to stay that way forever. That first summer I took a night class in computer science, which is how I met Glenn.

Like me, Glenn was a returning student, though several years younger and considerably less focused. But he was cute, funny and quite easy-going, an ambling Type B personality to temper my monomaniacal Type A. I will never forget how, on our first date, he had to shovel armloads of junk and trash from the front passenger seat of his Plymouth Duster so that I would have a place to sit. As he held the door for me and I slid into the seat, he said, "My grade point average is 3.8. What's yours?" I waited until he had closed the door and walked around to the driver's side before responding simply, "4.0."

On our second date, we shared a romantic dinner at a restaurant called Oliver's in Orange County. It had a Dickens motif, and Glenn had chosen it because he knew I would appreciate the literary aspect. I really liked him. And he had made it clear that he was attracted to me as well. So after we ate, I felt compelled to provide him with a lengthy explanation of how I had come to be a single mom trying to get an education while raising four children, how those two goals were my primary focus in life and would be for the next four years. I went on to tell him that my children had a father, flawed as he was, and I wasn't looking for a replacement, though anyone who would be with me would have to like kids, at least on some fundamental level. After a half hour or so of this, Glenn finally drawled, in his slow, Southern Texas manner, "Well, darlin', I hadn't really intended on proposin' tonight." He grinned, and I felt like an idiot. But our cards were on the table, and I made plans to have him over for dinner so he could meet my kids.

They liked him, which was a good sign (though he did show up bearing candy bars and other decadent treats for them). And so a new dimension was added to our lives. At twenty-eight, Glenn was really just a big kid himself. He enjoyed riding bikes or Rollerblading with us, and he loved to read, so he really just fit right into the family. When the school year started in the fall, Glenn and I were able to plan a couple of classes together. Doing so turned out to be a serendipitous boon to him, as I was able to help him keep up with his studies after he ended up in the hospital halfway through the semester.

Glenn owned a condominium in nearby Montclair, and he enjoyed doing home improvement projects. One night as we were talking on the phone, he mentioned that he'd been having pain in his knee, that it was red and swollen, no doubt because he'd been on his knees all day, putting new flooring in the kitchen. The next day on campus I could tell that he really was in a great deal of pain. Taking drugstore pain medication didn't seem to help at all. That afternoon he made an appointment with his physician—the family doctor he'd had while growing up. The elderly gentleman drained some fluid from his knee and sent him on his way, telling him to take aspirin and the problem would clear up in a day or two. When it didn't, Glenn went back to him, and the knee was drained again. After ten days, the knee and surrounding leg were swollen, red and warm to the touch. Glenn finally went to see his mother, a registered nurse, who took him immediately to see an orthopedic surgeon. At the end of that long day I received a phone call from Glenn informing me that he had been admitted to USC Medical Center and was awaiting emergency surgery. Doctors suspected an infection in his knee had led to grangrene. Their suspicions were correct.

Late that evening Glenn's knee was incised, the tissue which had been destroyed by the prolonged, untreated infection was removed, and the wound was bandaged but left open for direct, on-going treatment. For the first few days, the kindly young interns at this teaching hospital discussed amputation. Gangrene, if it is not arrested in time, can prove fatal. To save his life, Glenn's doctors considered amputating his leg just above the knee so that they could be certain he would not succumb to the putrid infection. Glenn was an athlete. When I met him, he was in amazing physical condition because he hit the gym twice a day, morning and night. And he loved to run. Though we did not discuss it, I know he told his doctors that he would rather die than lose his leg. I believe they took him seriously, as they made every effort over those crucial first days to make sure he was given the best care.

At the end of a long week, they told him that his body was doing a fine job of healing itself, and they were nearly ready to close the wound. Three days later, they released him. But he could not go home, they told him. Crutches would be mandatory for weeks, and only for short trips to the restroom; he was to stay off his feet the majority of the time, resting with the bad leg elevated. In a brief conversation, we discussed his options. He would stay with me until he was able to get around on his own.

My daily routine suddenly became a bit more complicated. Now, in addition to getting the kids ready for school in the morning, I was helping Glenn get to the restroom, making sure he was set for the day before I left. Since we had taken several classes together, I was able to explain to his teachers that he would return as soon as his doctors would allow him to, and that I would be taking notes for him, explaining lectures and turning in assignments for him. We made it work, and eventually he was able to return to school (albeit on crutches), and he actually maintained his B+ grade point average that semester.

He was still a long way from being able to use his leg, however, and so he was unable to return to his part-time job working in a luggage store. Immediately after his surgery, his boss told him she would hold the job open for him, that he should take as long as he needed to before returning. Unfortunately, his boss was a former girlfriend, and when she discovered he was staying with me, she fired him.

I will admit, I did experience some trepidation at the realization that I had an unemployed man with a gimpy leg lying about on my couch for a good part of every day. But Glenn was bright, charming and capable. It wasn't long before he was working again, this time at a health food store and for a boss who was sympathetic to his need to sit on a stool when he was behind the counter.

Slowly, ever so slowly, Glenn was able to walk again without the crutches. He used a brace, and he walked with a pronounced limp, but he was beginning to get around pretty well. And as soon as he could walk, he wanted to run.

In the six months since his surgery, he had gained fifty pounds. After overhearing a few clipped remarks from his mother, I realized that the ripped fit guy I'd fallen for had a tendency to carry extra weight. A lot of extra weight. He was barely getting around independently before his mother began to badger him about losing the weight he'd gained. Glenn was a man of big appetites. And he wasn't about to cut back on the amount of food he was consuming. He admitted that his fitness regimen of twice-daily gym workouts had begun when he'd needed to decrease his size.

The block we lived on in Chino Hills was a half mile long. Glenn decided one day that he would simply jog around the block. I suggested we simply walk it together. He was determined to run. By the time he returned, his body was drenched in sweat, and he was crying from the pain in his leg and the anger and frustration he felt at being in such a weakened state after he'd worked so hard to be at a top level of fitness. I knew that he was depressed as well. His unspoken fear was that he would never be able to run normally again. His dream of one day running a marathon or competing in a triathlon seemed to have dissolved in the light of this new day.

For some time, I could not console him. But as he stubbornly continued his daily attempt to jog around the block, he began to make progress in tiny increments. Eventually, he was able to make it all the way around the block without stopping, although it was more like a half-limp, half jog.

By then, we had completed a second semester of school. For me, that meant two years down, two more to go to earn the bachelor's degree. In the fall, I would be starting classes at the University of California, Riverside. As the kids finished school for the year and summer came on, I felt especially blessed and grateful.

We played again, this time with even greater insouciance than the summer before. Glenn's check helped pay the rent so I had less anxiety about finances. We went on many long, leisurely bike rides, which helped to rehabilitate Glenn's leg. We cooked outside on the barbecue almost every night. We rented movies and engaged in epic water battles. For all intents and purposes, we resembled an all-American family. The only thing missing was the family dog.

In September of 1986, I entered UC Riverside as a transfer student. Because I had earned straight A's at Chaffey College for two years, I was awarded a Watkins scholarship, which paid one hundred percent of my tuition. With the kids attending local schools, my mornings were less hectic. I made sure everyone was off to school on time, then drove to Riverside for a full day of classes. Most of my general education classes had been completed at the community college, so I was able now to begin work on my major, English, in earnest. I sat in the front in every class—which would have been entirely unlike me in high school, to say the least—and hung on every word of my professors. Between classes, I would walk in the botanical gardens, or retreat to a small courtyard with stone benches and ivy-covered walls next to the library, there to read the works of Keats or Yeats or Frost, immersing myself in a newfound love of poetry.

UCR was on the quarter system, so that three or four weeks in, I would find myself facing a grueling midterm based on hundreds of pages of reading. Then, in another month, I would take the final exam. I would walk in early, blue books and erasable pens in hand, write for three hours on an English final, nearly always one of the last to leave. At the end of my first quarter, I earned straight A's again, further boosting my sense of empowerment.

The only aspect of my education I found daunting at this point in time was the massive reading load. I'm sure that reading hundreds of pages a week was a reasonable goal for a young college student with little else to do (other than search for the current party on campus), but for a single woman raising four children while trying to maintain a romantic relationship, the rigor could be challenging, as noted in an excerpt from my journal of that time:

14 Nov 1986 10:37p.m.

It is on days like today that being a mother (and a lover) really tests the fabric of my being. I feel as though I am being pulled in five directions at once. Each child wants my time and attention in a different way, and my lover does his share of gentle pulling as well. I want to accommodate each of them, but that would only be possible if I could divide myself into five equal parts—or make four clones (not a bad idea). There are five of them and only one of me, and on days like today I feel like they are tearing me to shreds. I have to be flexible, to stretch myself as far as I dare, and then I have to be resilient enough to snap back to myself again. I have to be careful that I don't spread myself out so thin that I lose all of my warmth. And I have to stay soft. What are mothers made of? I think the fabric must be similar to what Superman's costume was made out of: something indestructible and extremely comfortable at the same time.

My emotions then often swept from contentment to elation to guilt to frustration and back again within a short amount of time. I knew that by getting an education I was doing what was best for the kids in the long run, and I loved the process, but often I longed to return to the slower, calmer days of being a stay-at-home mom. What I needed most in those days was more time, always more time—to play with the kids, to relax with Glenn, to read the literature I loved. Where I found time was in giving up sleep, unfortunately, functioning on no more than five or six hours on most nights.

Since going back to school, I also had little time to write, though occasionally, in a burst of creative energy, I would produce a story or an essay other than my required assignments for school. In three years I'd sold two children's stories to *Child Life* and *Jack & Jill* and a short personal essay to a cycling magazine. The money helped, and I longed to return more fully to the writing life, but I knew that would only happen when I'd found a good day job.

Again the school year sped by and again we celebrated the coming of summer, the season that brought with it time to rest, time to play, time to read (for pleasure, though I always took at least one summer school class). With each passing year, my stress and anxiety diminished somewhat as I grew closer to graduation. Though our financial resources were still very limited, we'd never gone without a meal, something I always feared I would subject my children to. With the summer of 1987 came the realization that at the end of the next school year, I would receive my diploma. The following year I would student teach, and then begin my career as a teacher. Finally, I began to relax just a bit, to slow down and savor what was left of my sojourn as a student. My attitude changed; I was less stressed out that summer. And in calming down somewhat, I began to reflect, which is, I'm sure, what caused me to end up at a local animal shelter one August afternoon.

It had been ten years since I'd lost Sapo. I still missed her every day. Glenn and I saw people with dogs whenever we hiked up into the hills or rode mountain bikes or just walked around the block together. Most of our neighbors had dogs. Our landlord had a "no pets" rule in the lease, but he wasn't very strict, and we had taken good care of his property. Glenn had spent time trimming trees, planting honeysuckle along the chain link fence, repairing the lawn sprinklers and weeding around the rose bushes in the courtyard. The place looked less like a rental and more like a real home. I was pretty certain the landlord wouldn't mind us having a dog.

But I had reservations. Was it fair to my children to take on the expense of a dog when I had already denied them so much? On the other hand, was it fair to them to grow up without the companionship of a family dog? What if I brought a dog home, the kids fell in love with it, but the landlord objected? These concerns riffed through my mind for days on end. One day while the kids were off having an adventure and Glenn was at work, I found myself at the City of Upland animal shelter.

The place was austere, to say the least, and not very spacious. There was a small section for cats, and then a larger section of the building that housed stray dogs in cement and chain link kennels. I told myself I would "just look," to see what kind of dogs were available. In my heart I knew that I was hoping to find a dog like Sapo. I also knew I had to let that thought go in order to be willing to open my heart to another dog, just as I'd had to open my heart to Sapo after losing Ruf. Mostly, walking through the kennels just made me sad.

I was almost ready to leave when I saw a dog curled in a ball at the back of a kennel. She was gray and white, marked like a husky, but she was mixed with some short-haired breed. I knelt by the door to the kennel and called her. She uncurled slowly and walked over to me, tail between her legs in submission. Her face was beautiful but her ears were lowered in defeat and her eyes were glazed with fear, suspicion and something else, something ineffable that indicated a wildness about her. I wanted to rescue her, to get her out of that cage and into some place of safety. But her demeanor gave the impression that she would not be the playful, affectionate dog Sapo had been, which was the kind of dog I now wanted to provide for my children. This dog seemed detached in some primal way, and so I moved on and continued down the row, stepping aside for a very large woman and several children. The husky mix sat by her kennel door, looking after me. When the children saw her, they began to exclaim loudly to their mother, and the woman responded shrilly in a voice several decibels above theirs, "Oh look at the pretty doggie! Isn't she pretty?" I turned to see the poor dog retreat quickly to the back of the kennel. She began to tremble as the children jumped and squealed outside her cage. I found myself walking with determined steps toward the lobby. When I returned with an animal control officer, we had to gently push our way through the crowd of kids. The big woman glared at me as the officer clipped a leash on the cowering dog and brought her out. I heard the kids whine in disappointment as their mother commanded them to look at other dogs.

Outside, on a small patch of green lawn in the fresh, quiet air, the dog calmed a bit and stopped trembling. The officer told me she'd been picked up as a stray in the foothills of Upland. She was young, not yet spayed, and had probably wandered from home when she began her first estrus. She sat quietly beside me, then looked up into my eyes. I could see the long-ing there, her plea to be liberated from this frighten-ing captivity, to be given a chance to be someone's beloved dog. No way could I leave her behind.

A short time later, she was sitting quietly in the passenger seat of my car.

"What shall we call you?" I mused aloud. I had learned my lesson with Sapo; names are important and the choosing of such should not be left to careless jest or frivolity. I remembered a movie my sister and I had loved as kids. "Nikki, Wild Dog of the North" was one of many great nature-adventure films created by Disney before the days of epic animated features. The star of the movie was a Malamute, much huskier than my current passenger, but with the same beautiful face and markings.

"Is that what you are, Girl? Are you a Malamute?" I knew she was definitely one of the wilder breeds. One look in her eyes told that story. In the previous quarter at school, I had taken a Russian studies class and had been reading a lot of Solzhenitsyn, Tolstoy and Dos-toyevsky, among other beloved Russian authors. I am intrigued by the use of long, formal Russian names which always include a short diminutive for family and close friends. (Thus Lara's full name in Dr. Zhivago is Larisa Feodorovna Guishar.) "Nikki" seemed like a good fit, but a dog with these eyes that spoke of wild, faraway places needed a more formal name. Consider-ing all of my favorite Russians, I came up with Nikita Feodorovna Baryshnikov Zhivago—"Niki" for short.

CHAPTER EIGHT

I can't recall the details of how I introduced Niki to my children (though I did use all four of her names). I do remember distinctly that Shali, now fifteen, was not pleased at having been left out of the decision making. But she quickly forgot about being miffed as she allowed herself to be sniffed and greeted by our beautiful new family member.

My decision had been so spontaneous that I had made no provision for a dog—I needed dog food, a real collar and leash and some dishes for her. So we left her in the backyard for a quick trip to the store. I didn't think Glenn would be home before we got back, but just in case, I left him a note. It read something like:

Went to the store—be right back. My friend Niki is in the backyard. Please make her feel welcome!

It was at this point in time that I learned a very critical lesson in bonding.

Glenn's truck was in the driveway when we returned from the store. We found him in the back yard, sprawled on his back in the grass with Niki stretched out beside him, her head resting on his chest. The look in her eyes had changed from fear to abject adoration as she stared into his face. My dog was in love with my boyfriend.

I hadn't really discussed getting a dog with Glenn. I didn't know how he would feel about it, and I didn't want to be influenced by whatever he would say. It was my decision, I felt, because the dog would be my dog. I had not counted on "my dog" falling in love with him, but she did, and that was that. The kids and I had been unable to convince Niki that it was safe to come inside the house. In a short time, Glenn had coaxed her in. She stuck by his side like Rufus had stuck to mine.

Within days after Niki came home, Glenn decided he wanted to take her on a jog. It had been nearly two years since his knee surgery, and though he had recovered enough to run without limping, he was still very heavy and very slow. I tried to talk him out of taking her as I just didn't know if it would be healthy for her. He pointed out that she'd probably run for miles in the foothills before her capture, and that she was far more fit than he was.

"Let's just see how it goes," he said. And off they went.

Turns out, he was right; her level of fitness was far beyond his. Once she understood what they were doing, he told me later, she ran out to the end of the leash and led him all the way around the block, pulling just enough to make him increase his speed ever so slightly.

"She made me run a personal best," he said, delighted.

Thus began an era in our lives, inspired by Nikita's love of running. Glenn began to time himself on every run, going farther each time and gradually increasing his speed. Initially, I fretted over Niki a great deal, checking her foot pads whenever they returned from a long run, insisting that she stay home if temperatures outside were particularly warm. But Glenn took good care of her, sometimes stopping in to drop her off at the house if he wanted to run longer and he felt she was beginning to tire, and he never ran her on asphalt, only on the smooth concrete of the sidewalk.

I began to run more often myself, sometimes following behind my man and my—his—dog as they ran. My boys got in on the action, running laps around the block with us and sometimes farther. Eventually they would run—and win—2K races held in conjunction with 5 and 10K races Glenn and I would compete in as he began to train for the Los Angeles Marathon. He was losing weight and gaining fitness with his new running partner, and I envied them. I had meant to find a dog companion for myself. I'd succeeded in finding one for Glenn.

We didn't always run. Occasionally, early on the weekend mornings, Glenn and I would leave my children slumbering and we would walk up into the hills behind the housing tract, letting Niki off the leash to run like a wild dog up and down the chaparral-covered slopes. She would often desert us for long minutes, chasing after squirrels or rabbits, reappearing with a happy dog face and panting tongue. On one such morning, Niki vanished into the foliage, heading up a hill next to the trail as we walked along. Seconds later we saw her fifty yards away but directly in front of us, sitting on another slope, calmly watching us. "She must be a magician," one of us remarked, and we called her to come back to us. But she didn't move, just sat quietly watching us. After calling a second time, we realized simultaneously that the dog we were seeing was not Niki, and it was not a dog at all, it was a coyote. In the faint dawn light, with its absence of color, the 'yote looked just like her. We panicked for a moment, calling Niki loudly until she ran up behind us. She had been close by all along. We looked at her, looked at the coyote and chuckled. No wonder her ears were so big; Niki was a coyote-dog mix, or "coydog." Some time after this incident, we happened to be at a small local zoo that had a poor, agitated coyote in a small enclosure. As it paced, I took a photo, which we compared to a photo of Niki stretched out on our bed. With the exception of coloring, the two were identical. At last we understood the wild look in her eyes and her tendency to sit up tall, raise her muzzle to the sky in classic coyote fashion and let loose a hair-raising howl when she heard a fire or police siren. It also explained some other interesting behaviors she had, including denning. From the first night home, she preferred to sleep in the closet. We had given her a mound of old blankets to sleep on, including an old down comforter. When we heard her scratching around deep at one end of a long closet, we thought she might need to go outside. It took the humans a little while to comprehend that she was pushing things around, making herself a den. We brought her out and showed her the lovely bed we'd made for her, but she simply took the first opportunity to dive back into the closet, shoving shoes out of the way with her nose, circling around and around. We gave in and threw down a blanket where she seemed to want it. Her den in the closet became her safe place for retreat during thunderstorms and other frightening experiences (such as visiting relatives). We understood more fully her need for 'wild time' in the hills, and we tried to accommodate her whenever we could, although we watched her more closely with the realization that her coyote cousins were so close. She always returned from these adventures calm and content, bringing home on her fur the pleasant aroma of wild sage.

Niki was funny and sweet and beautiful, and she was wholly bonded to Glenn. Watching the two together deepened the longing I had for my own best-dog-friend. I envied their companionship, the partnership they displayed when they ran together. Niki's devotion to Glenn mirrored what Sapo's had been with me, and I wondered if the pain of losing her would ever diminish. Sapo had helped me heal after losing Rufus. I had hoped that Niki would provide a similar unconditional love. She did, but not for me.

And so, with another summer and my college graduation fast approaching, I found myself back at the Upland animal shelter one balmy spring morning while the kids were at school.

I had nearly a déjà vu experience in coming upon a dog curled at the back of the kennel as Niki had been, a dog whose sad brown eyes reflected not the same fear and anxiety she had shown, but rather a sadness that had reached heart-breaking depths. It was with a long, heavy sigh that this dog moved toward me from the back of the kennel.

Dogs in shelters will often exhibit behaviors which are not typical for them in familiar surroundings. They may pace nervously or bark in excitement or growl and act aggressively out of fear. Dogs, like humans, are individuals, and each will respond to incarceration in his or her own way, according to personality and circumstances. Few are calm and placid. This one was.

I asked about him at the front desk and was told he'd been at the shelter for over a month and that a local rescue group had agreed to fund his care. Otherwise, he would have been euthanized when he wasn't quickly adopted.

A shelter worker followed me back to the kennel, clipped a leash on the dog's collar, and led him outside to a small plot of grass where he spent most of his time relieving himself. She told me he was obviously housebroken, as he would only go when someone took him outside.

"He's a good dog," she sighed, "but no one wants him because he's big and, well, black." Black dogs, like black cats, have a harder time finding adoptive homes.

I took the leash from her and walked him up and down, then sat with him on the grass for awhile. I thought he must be an older dog, given his calm demeanor and good behavior. The truth is, he had simply become resigned to his life behind bars. He wasn't really a calm dog at all, in the sense of being passive or unengaged. In reality, he was depressed.

"I'll take him," I told the woman at the front counter. I let her know that I had another dog at home. If the two could get along, all would be fine. If not, I would have to bring him back. I was pretty certain there would be no problem. After some paperwork was quickly dispatched, I opened the back hatch of my Plymouth station wagon and the big black dog jumped in. While he lay in the back of the car, panting heavily and drooling copiously, I drove us home, wondering how he would get along with the new sister he would find there.

I thought he was about the same size as Niki, but when I got him home, I realized he was much bigger. I brought him into the backyard through a side gate and unclipped his leash. As he trotted around, examining the perimeter of the yard (and marking it frequently), I began to notice more about him. He had the brown 'eyebrows' and other brown markings of a Rottweiler, but his hair was thick and long. His tail curled over his back, and his tongue was mottled, black and pink—signs, my vet assured me later, that while one parent was clearly a Rottie, the other was apparently a Chow Chow. He had the small round feet of a Chow, a trait I found endearingly incongruous in this big solid tank of a dog.

When we let Niki out of the house to meet her new brother, the two sniffed noses and tails, and each concluded the other posed no threat. They quickly became good friends.

All that was left to do was name him, and I was stymied. Niki's name had come so easily. Nothing seemed to fit for this dog. I made a few suggestions, but they were immediately rebuffed by the kids. I thought, finally, that his name should somehow match with Niki's, so I settled for Aleksandr Solzhenitsyn—"Alex" for short—but I knew this name was far too lofty and formal for this shaggy pound puppy.

Glenn returned home from work during the process, assessed the new dog from afar, and remained quiet and noncommittal in his response.

Despite finding Alex at the same shelter in the same kennel where I found Niki, his homecoming had nothing of the fairy tale magic hers had. The kids were a bit intimidated by this big black male dog, and Glenn was clearly unimpressed as he watched Alex trot around the yard peeing on every recently planted vine and shrub. And I was secretly glad for this. I didn't want to lose my new dog's affection to Glenn's charisma, as I had with Niki, but it seems my anxiety was unwarranted in this regard. His tepid response was revealed tacitly in disapproving facial expressions, and my children seemed to echo his lack of enthusiasm. So much so, in fact, that I began to question my judgment about bringing Alex home. Niki was so beloved, no dog could compete, so perhaps it wasn't fair to bring him into a family that had already found the perfect dog. I waited to see what the next days would bring.

We left Alex outside for the first night. I had some trepidation about him marking territory, so to speak, in the house, so I left him in the backyard overnight. The next morning he met me at the back door, waving his huge fan of a tail. Later that day, a skateboarder rode noisily past the yard, and Alex barked at him. Initially, I moved to reprimand him, but then realized happily that he was simply protecting his yard, his family, and I praised him for doing so. Throughout the day, he followed Niki in and out of the house with no mishaps, so we allowed him to sleep inside that night. He stretched out on the floor beside the bed, sighed heavily, and settled his big head down on his little round paws. I didn't hear another sound out of him all night.

On the weekend, the boys wanted to ride their bikes up into the hills. Usually when we did this, Niki would trot easily along beside Glenn on his bike until we were well away from the housing tract, then he would release her from the leash and let her run. Taking Alex was another experience altogether. He moved in all directions, crossing in front of the bike or pulling me off to the side. We struggled up the road in fits and starts, finally achieving the top of the hill that overlooked our tract. We hadn't gone far before Alex simply collapsed in the dirt. I realized too late that the heat of the warm spring day combined with his lack of overall fitness had taken its toll. "He's overheating," I told Glenn with a pang of guilt. I didn't know how I would manage to get him home in his condition. I couldn't carry him; he was simply too big for me.

Moments later the boys found a deep hole that had been dug by a backhoe as part of a large construction project (one which would eventually obstruct our view with new homes). A foot or so of rainwater left over from a recent storm stagnated in the bottom of the hole, and we gently urged Alex toward it. He approached tentatively at first, then discovered, as he stepped in with his dainty feet, how refreshing the water felt, and he thrust his whole body in, wading through the slimy muck and lapping it up as he went. I worried he would become ill from the water or the heat, so I left Glenn to ride with the boys, and I took Alex home.

He smelled awful. On our romps with Niki, she always returned home smelling sweetly of wild foliage. Alex smelled like sour algae mixed with stale dog urine, vestiges left over from the animal shelter.

"No way you're coming in the house smelling like that, Pal," I told him.

A bath was in order. Using the backyard garden hose and my inexpensive shampoo, I scrubbed him clean, pulling away long strands of tangled black hair in the process. The yard was a mess of dog hair, muddy grass and dirty soap suds when I finished, and my back ached from bending over him for so long, but finally a clean, sweetly scented dog stood before me. I toweled him off, then unclipped his leash. Through the washing process, he had stood stoically, looking up at me with his sad but now trusting brown eyes. When I set him free, he hesitated only briefly before barreling around the yard in circles, stopping occasionally to roll on his back or rub his snout along the grass in an attempt to lose some of the girl smell and retrieve as much of the outdoor smell as he could. It was the first time I'd seen him exhibit any kind of behavior that could be classified as happy.

"Alex!" I called to him, laughing. He ran straight at me, charging into my knees and knocking me to the ground before resuming his mad chase around the yard.

"Damn it, Alex," I admonished him as I examined a large bruise on my knee. "You're too big!" This phrase would be repeated often in times to come, sometimes in exasperation, but more and more out of fondness... though it took awhile.

Our next challenge was a run together, which went about as smoothly as the bike ride had.

I guess I expected Alex to easily comprehend what I wanted, as Niki had done so beautifully with Glenn. I will not concede that she was smarter. Alex's thought processes just worked differently than hers did. If I had been a faster runner, I might have been able to get him to adapt more quickly by making him run to stay up with me. But the best I could do on a good day was a slow jog, which didn't even resemble that, the first time we tried it. Much like the bike ride, Alex would dart off here and there, to sniff, pee, watch, wag and sniff (and pee) again. He couldn't go more than a few feet without cutting me off. A quarter mile into the run, he cut me off abruptly, tripping me with the leash. My knees and hands slammed into the concrete of the sidewalk. I returned home—limping slowly—in tears of pain and frustration. Glenn just shook his head and made an unkind remark about the intelligence level of my dog. His words angered me. It wasn't Alex's fault. He simply didn't understand yet what I was trying to get him to do. And while Niki loved to run, Alex loved to meander. Hers was the personality of the wild hunter. His was more like Ferdinand the bull; he was content to sit and smell the flowers.

I didn't give up, and I discovered that a quick tug on the leash and a brusque "Hey!" would help him get back on track when he began to lose focus. In turn, he learned that if he paid attention and concentrated on the run, he would have time to stroll around leisurely and visit all the trees on the front parkway after we finished. It took time, but we became a good team, and I appreciated his company on my runs, as by this time Glenn—with Niki's help—had increased his pace to such an extent that we couldn't run together any more. In all honesty, I didn't really enjoy running; I did it to ameliorate the stress in my life and for the sake of my overall fitness. I knew I needed to run, even if I didn't want to, and having Alex by my side made me less bored as I ran. I took to tying a bandana around his neck each time we ran, choosing a color that would match whichever running togs I happened to be wearing. Alex, always the good-natured soul, never complained.

As he ran more, Alex became healthier, shedding some of the fat he'd gained while languishing at the pound. And each time we ran, our bond grew stronger. We had not experienced the immediate love-at-first-sight that Glenn and Niki had. But as Alex and I spent time together, we became good friends, then close companions. In time, he shadowed me everywhere when I was at home.

In the beginning, Alex had been so listless and depressed, I had concluded from his lack of energy that he must be an older dog. But at his first check up with our family vet, Dr. Chung, I learned that he was in fact still a puppy, not even a year old. I had been treating him as if he were a sedate, middle-aged dog. When I realized how young he was, I tried to romp and play with him more. I bought him chew toys and balls to play with. It was a gradual process, as if he had to recover from whatever sadness he'd left behind at the shelter, but eventually he became more playful. The first time he looked at me expectantly, wanting to play, his ears perked and his eyebrows raised in an expectant expression, I knew this great goofy dog had my heart. One day as I gazed at him fondly I called him by his full name—and knew it just didn't fit.

"You're just not Aleksandr Solzhenitsyn," I told him. "You're...." And in a flash, it came to me. "Alex Haley." The beloved author, one of my heroes in life, was round and personable, just like my Alex. The name fit perfectly. And so it was that my Alex became Alex Haley, and one day he would prove himself to be my hero as well.

My last quarter of school at UC Riverside had been bittersweet. I looked forward to wearing a cap and gown, to achieving my goal and receiving my bachelor's degree. But I dreaded leaving the comfort zone of college. I loved everything I was learning, and I was in no hurry to turn the tables and have to be the one preparing lectures and lesson plans.

In class one day in the last weeks of school, a young woman I'd gotten to know as a classmate confided that she was looking into graduate school.

"Everyone assumes an English major will teach," she mused. "But there are other careers out there. I'm thinking of going to law school."

Her casual comment subtly, almost imperceptibly at first, changed the direction of the wind in my sails. Over the next few days, I reflected on what she'd said, and I began to share my thoughts with Glenn. Teaching would afford me the greatest amount of time with my kids, and I would have summers off to write. But the girls were already in high school, Ezra in junior high and Sam not far behind. In a few short years, the kids would leave home to pursue their own college educations and careers. I had been single-minded and relentless in my drive to complete my education so that I could provide for them. But how long would they need me to do so? And wouldn't I be able to provide for them in a much grander way if I chose a more lucrative career than teaching high school English?

I couldn't get the idea of law school out of my head. It was something I would never have considered four years before when I enrolled in my first classes at Chaffey, hoping to slide by with C's. In a few weeks, I would graduate from the University of California with honors. With one exception, I had never earned less than an A on any English paper I'd ever written, and my work had been included in UCR's prestigious literary journal, *Ideas of Order*. I would emerge from my undergraduate studies as a different person from the anxious, intimidated girl I once was. I had become a much stronger woman, confident in myself, appreciative of the knowledge I'd gained in all subjects, not just English. I wanted to choose a path for my life that honored those feelings.

I had also spent some time thinking about the legacy of my father. He'd been a cop in Highland Park, Illinois, just outside of Chicago. But when he and Mom moved to California, he'd taken a job as a night watchman. He worked the swing shift, leaving in the afternoon to go to work and coming home in the middle of the night to sleep for a few hours before rising early to head off to law school. He studied part time, finished, passed the bar exam—and soon after was diagnosed with the illness that would take his life. Goaded on by the lofty and romantic ambition of completing his dream, I contacted Western State University College of Law in nearby Fullerton and was asked to come in for an interview.

I was accepted by the dean of Western State at the end of that interview before I'd even filled out the application, on the condition that I passed the Law School Admissions Test. Two weeks later I took the LSAT—the most challenging exam I've ever taken— and my score missed qualifying me for financial aid by one point. Still, it was beyond sufficient to get me in, and with a student loan to cover tuition, I made plans to begin law school in the fall.

On a swelteringly hot day near the first day of summer, my family gathered in our back yard in Chino Hills for my graduation party. I felt relieved and elated simultaneously, and thrilled to make the announcement that I would be heading on to law school. It was an amazing day, the culmination of so much sacrifice and so little sleep, and I allowed myself—for once—to slow down and bask in the joy of it.

I tried to hold that memory close a few short weeks later as I spent nearly $500 on books and attended Western State's orientation. Two thirds of students in the first year of law school drop out, we were reminded. I didn't want to become a statistic, and I resolved to study hard and do what it took, once again, to earn top grades. I did get decent grades, finishing the semester with a B+ average. But the toll it took on me and my family was more than I could have imagined.

The challenge with law school does not come from trying to understand and apply the law. My logical mind had little difficulty with that aspect of it, and in fact, I loved the study of the law and writing memoranda. The challenge for most students is keeping up with the work load. Not only does this require reading hundreds of pages of case history every week, but it is also necessary to write out a brief of the case so that if one is called upon in class, an intelligent defense of the disposition of the case may ensue.

Every night after classes I sat at the desk in my bedroom, isolated from the rest of the family, reading cases and writing briefs long into the night. I missed my kids. I missed spending time with Glenn. I became exhausted, then ill with some sort of respiratory infection. I was just beginning to feel better one Saturday when Glenn had a 10K race he wanted me to attend with him. I didn't feel up to it, but I felt so guilty for being consumed by school that I went. In the chill morning, I sat in his truck, waiting for him to finish the race. By the time he was ready to head home, I had begun having chest pains every time I inhaled. Over the next hour, the pain would become nearly unbearable. Glenn took me to the emergency room, and I was diagnosed with pleurisy, an infection of the lining surrounding the lungs. For three days, I was so sick and in so much pain I only got up to use the bathroom, and so weak that I needed help getting there.

When finally I began to feel better, I was immediately overwhelmed with how far behind I'd gotten in my studying. One evening as I sat at my desk, forcing myself to concentrate on a case concerning contract law, I heard the whisper of a sigh. I turned in my chair to see my seven-year-old son sitting in the doorway, his back leaning against the door jam.

"Hey, Sam, what's up?" I asked. I will never forget his heartrending tone as he replied.

"Well, I was gonna ask you to play with me. But you're studying. So I'm just going to sit here with you."

I had to turn my chair away so he would not see my tears.

The next day I went to the dean's office and told him I would be withdrawing from school at the semester. "I love the study of law," I told him. "But I am the only parent my children have. Their needs have to come before anything else." Sam's plaintive resignation to simply sit in my presence reminded me of what I'd once felt after my father died and my mother started heading to the bar instead of coming home after work. I felt absolutely alone in the world, with no one to care for me. I couldn't bear the thought of Sam feeling that way. I would make many sacrifices for my education, but I wasn't willing to sacrifice the well-being of my kids.

I applied and was accepted to UC Riverside's teacher credentialing program, but classes would not start until the following September, so I spent the next months substitute teaching. Turns out, I enjoyed it far more than I ever thought I would. I had looked forward to teaching as I had looked forward to starting college—with a fair amount of trepidation, and for the same reason; I just didn't think I'd be very good at it. But I'd been wrong on both counts. I subbed every subject at every level, from Kindergarten to twelfth grade. I enjoyed the work because I enjoyed the kids. At every age, I found them delightfully innocent and imaginative, in the same way that I was entertained on a daily basis by my own kids' comical antics and unique perspective on the world.

When September rolled around, I was back in school again at my beloved alma mater, and I jumped in with both feet, eager to get the preliminaries out of the way so I could begin my student teaching. As it turned out, I was hired as an intern teacher three months into the program—my first position in my new career. That school year was impossibly challenging at times. I drove thirty-three miles from Chino Hills to a middle school in San Bernardino five days a week, leaving the house at 5:30a.m. On Tuesdays, Thursdays and Fridays I had evening classes to attend, so I drove from San Bernardino to Riverside after work, then finally home late in the evening, a total of seventy-six miles of driving in one day. The schedule was grueling. But I knew it was only temporary, and I promised my children that things would get easier. They did. Before I'd completed my credential work, I was offered a position as an English teacher at newly built Jurupa Valley High School in Mira Loma. It would be the second high school for Jurupa Unified School District. The first was Rubidoux, my high school alma mater. Construction was underway on JVHS during the time that I'd been subbing, and on one fine Saturday morning I had asked Glenn to drive me over to the site with our bikes in the back of his truck. As I rode circles around the campus, dodging large trucks and piles of building materials strewn around the freshly paved parking lot (which once was a field I'd ridden my horse through), I placed my claim to the Universe.

"You owe me!" I shouted exuberantly to the heavens as I sat astride my bright yellow mountain bike, a graduation gift from Glenn's father. "I lived through hell here!" Glenn, never much ruffled by my eccentricities, looked on.

And so I found myself returning once again to Mira Loma in September of 1990, this time to meet my new

CHAPTER NINE

Something surprising occurred the night I signed all those papers for my new health care plan with the school district. I don't recall how the conversation began, but Glenn—for the first time in our five years together—brought up "the M word." (That's actually how he referred to it; he had taken me at my word not to discuss marriage until I'd finished school and embarked on a career that would enable me to support my children. A few times he had told his mother, "We don't talk about the M word.")

We'd made reservations for dinner at a really nice restaurant in Orange County, just the two of us. It had been years since we'd gone out to an upscale place. We simply couldn't afford it before. After signing all the paperwork for my new job, we would celebrate. Before we went to dinner, Glenn began to pontificate on the benefits of legal partnership. He mentioned how long it had been since he'd had his teeth cleaned or his vision tested. He also made reference to an on-going problem with his feet; he'd run the L.A. Marathon the previous spring and his feet had been bothering him ever since. He had no medical insurance, which is why he'd ended up at USC's teaching hospital when his knee became infected.

The conversation continued at the restaurant, and at some point I pulled a small notepad out of my handbag and created two columns on a page—one for pros and one for cons. The pros were tax breaks, mutual insurance benefits and (on my part) the opportunity to make a legal name change from Denny's last name to Glenn's. The cons were having to get a blood test (Glenn's), long-term commitment (Glenn again, I'm afraid) and taking on the financial responsibility of the other partner (mine, definitely mine).

None of this bore any resemblance to a romantic proposal. It constituted the logical, analytical contemplation of two people who'd survived family stress (including the occasional misdeeds of a neurotic, vindictive ex-husband—details to be revealed posthumously from the pages of my journals), financial stress, time stress and co-habiting with burgeoning adolescents while still somehow, miraculously managing to salvage some affection for each other.

We would have added "expense of a wedding" to the con side, but as I explained to Glenn, for the next several years, any "extra" money I made would be going to the needs of my children to make up for our years of going without new clothes and other luxuries. He expressed only relief at that, since he'd been so nervous about his first wedding he'd gotten drunk early in the day and stayed that way throughout, just to be able to endure it. (Had I been the bride, such behavior would not have blessed me on my special day and was, in fact, a big reason they'd divorced less than a year later.)

We were enjoying a decadent dessert and some coffee when Glenn asked our waiter for a phone book.

"A telephone book, Sir?" was his incredulous response. But he brought one to the table several minutes later.

In looking up "Justice of the Peace" in the yellow pages, Glenn discovered that, for couples who were living together, no blood test was required. Scratch one off the con side. Which left one more pro than con.

We were married the next day.

I did ask my children first, and all four gave their blessings, though I realize doing so had more to do with pleasing me than what their own personal opinions of Glenn might be.

The fee for the service was $110. When the clerk asked how we would pay for it, Glenn looked at me, I suppose because I was the one with the new job, making me now the breadwinner of the family. I charged the amount to my brand new Visa card, with an admonishment to Glenn: "If you ever get stupid and leave me," I told him, "you agree to pay for the entire divorce." He agreed, and I asked the clerk to witness our verbal contract. (My one semester in law school has proven beneficial on more than one occasion in subsequent years.)

After a lively lunch with the kids, we returned home, and I began dutifully amending all those insurance forms to reflect my new name and my added insured family member.

Glenn and I were married on September 1, 1990. A week later, I began teaching high school. Generally, first year teachers have an overwhelming amount of work to do, but I had been hired in a newly created position meant to provide release time for the other English teachers on the faculty. Basically, I took over someone else's teaching duties for the day. Since I had subbed, I found it easy to move in and out of various grade levels and teaching styles, so that first year was nearly effortless. I had a golden opportunity to observe the teaching methods of some truly great veterans, and I had no lessons to plan myself, no homework assignments to grade. I loved my job, I loved my paychecks, and I loved my new husband.

Problem was, he didn't seem to be loving me in return.

In the first months after our fifteen-minute ceremony in front of the Justice of the Peace, Glenn seemed to drift away somehow, and I didn't really understand why. During my semester of law school, when I was away from home for long hours, then locked away studying when I was there, he'd been one hundred and ten percent supportive of me, never complaining, always willing to pitch in and help out, sometimes (to my embarrassment) boasting to his family about my future career. Things were different now. He seemed distracted, on edge. He was in his last year at Cal State Fullerton. I assumed he must be feeling anxious about school and what he would do after graduation, and I thought he would just work through these issues.

In April, Glenn's sister, Alesia, got married and I sang in her wedding. I hadn't sung at a public event in many years, and it felt good to be doing so. But during the reception, my husband disappeared for a long time. As I drove us home (because he'd had far too much to drink to be driving), he explained that he'd seen someone at the wedding he knew, a friend of his sister's that he'd dated for awhile in high school, and he'd enjoyed catching up with her. I didn't mind so much that he'd left me to go talk to another woman for a long period of time, except for the fact that this was atypical behavior for Glenn. He was generally pretty affectionate and almost clingy in his attention to me whenever we were out in public. At least, he was before we were married.

In May, Glenn's cousin also married, and we flew to Texas because, having heard me sing in Alesia's wedding, Robyn had asked if I would come out to sing in hers. The weekend was stressful to say the least, and ended in absolute disaster. We flew out on a Friday night. Glenn had been withdrawing from me more and more in recent weeks, and I foolishly thought the time alone together would enable us to restore some of our intimacy. He was sullen and taciturn on the flight out, however, and that attitude remained pervasive until the wedding reception, at which point he snapped at me angrily because I had insisted—in a lighthearted way— that he dance with his wife. His tone was one I'd never heard in the five and a half years we'd been together.

During the school year, we had sat through one of those tedious pitches to buy a time share, and as a result had "won" two nights' stay at the Imperial Palace in Las Vegas. When the school year ended in June, I convinced Glenn this would be the perfect opportunity for the honeymoon we'd never taken. In my mind, it would again be an opportunity to spend quality time alone together, to mend whatever tear had occurred in our relationship.

The day before we left for Vegas, we were discussing, in very civil, unemotional tones, what time we would leave the next morning. I wanted to hit the road early to avoid the heat and traffic. Glenn remarked that he had errands to do and wanted to leave later. When pressed, he admitted that his errand involved dropping off an application for a graduate program at Cal Poly Pomona. When I began teaching, I encouraged Glenn to cut back his work hours and increase the number of classes he was taking so that he could graduate by the end of the year. I told him I would make the financial commitment to get him through. It seemed logical to me that the sooner he graduated, the sooner he would be teaching as well, which was the career path he had chosen. That morning, he said that he'd realized how much he really liked school, and that he wanted to "keep going," so instead of applying to UCR's credential program, as he'd originally planned, he was going to begin work on a master's degree.

"And... so... what about working?" I asked. He replied that he was "not ready" to begin teaching yet, that he simply wanted to continue going to school as long as he could. I asked him to rethink his decision, given the fact that we—I—had children to support and had talked about buying our own home one day when we were finally a double-income family. The conversation ended there.

The next morning, without further discussion, Glenn drove out to Cal Poly before heading toward Vegas. We were both silent for hours. Finally, I asked him to talk to me about what had been bothering him for months. He responded with a speech that went on for miles. From his perspective, I had been the wet blanket thrown on his fun for years, disapproving every time he'd spent "his own money" to buy racing togs, cycling gear (including bicycles), inline skates (for training purposes) and a long list of other items necessary for his athletic endeavors. I replied with my own speech in an attempt to describe for him what it felt like to deny my children the pleasures of childhood—new bikes, new clothes, shoes whenever they were needed instead of only when a grant check came in—while watching him bring new toys home with every whim for something better or faster. He told me I was never fun. I told him I'd had to postpone fun until I could provide for my children. He asked me if he should turn the truck around, return home and move out. I told him we should not make hasty decisions, that perhaps the time away would give us a chance to work through our feelings, find common ground. He continued on to Vegas, but barely spoke to me while we were there and not at all on the drive home. Several weeks later, he moved out. We hadn't made it to our first anniversary.

Of course, there is far more to the story, as is the case with any break-up. In the months after Glenn moved out, he floated in and out of our lives, at times making overtures that indicated he wanted to come home, but I realized later—much, much later—that the truth of the matter was, he didn't want to file for divorce until he'd finished up with every medical and dental procedure he'd been able to take care of while still on my insurance. Friends and family members suggested he was using me. I just didn't want to believe it. Until the night he called to ask if I would teach him how to line dance—so he would be more successful in his efforts to pick up women at country bars. I agreed, and that night I watched him drink sixty dollars worth of alcohol in less than two hours. In his drunken state, he confessed that I was "the perfect wife," and our break-up had been entirely his fault, because he'd decided he wanted to return to the carefree life of a bachelor.

Two years after we'd begun to live entirely separate lives, he called to tell me he'd had his last tooth capped, and he would be filing for divorce in the near future. I reminded him of our contract. After a long pause, he grudgingly agreed that he "owed me" that much. A few nights later, he called again. He wanted to know if I intended to take back my maiden name. I hadn't really thought about it.

"It's going to cost me more if you do," he said.

"Absolutely," I replied. "I absolutely want to take back my maiden name." His response was a heavy sigh in acquiescence.

All of these events I find painfully difficult to divulge. For six years I had fooled myself into thinking that Glenn and I were building a life together. In hindsight, I was building a life for my children while Glenn was building a life for, well, Glenn. He never denied himself anything, now glaringly apparent in retrospect, evidenced by his many new toys and gadgets, his constant struggle with his weight. And I had denied myself so much. I told myself for years that everything would work out once I began teaching. In reality, everything unraveled.

I want to say that I had become a strong and independent woman, so I dealt with the break-up in a healthy way, accepting it as simply a new phase in life. In truth, it brought me to my knees emotionally, and I was thrust into a depression that weighted me down for over a year.

It wasn't the loss of Glenn that shook me so. Once he moved out, I immediately sensed an absence of the tension that had begun to build between him and my adolescent children. It was, once again, the loss of a dream. Just as my heart had broken when I realized Denny had no intention of carrying out the plans we had made for our future, so it broke again with the realization that all my promises to my children about having double-income parents who would make sure all their needs were met, take them on vacations and trips to Disneyland, had evaporated with his leaving. I was once again a single woman with four kids—four kids who deserved to have some good things happen in life. I felt as if I had failed them, and I didn't know how to make it right.

For months, I would come home from work and sit in one corner of the couch, emotionally detached from everyone and everything. Several experiences brought me out of my stupor, finally. It began when I allowed myself to express the full range of my emotions, from anger to disappointment to sorrow to yes, a bit of hope, over all of it, and my most authentic expression of these feelings came in my writing, in long journal entries which chronicled our relationship and everything I thought had gone wrong. As time went on, I wrote less about the catastrophe, more about my own personal growth and how I wanted to structure my life in the future.

And I ran. Sometimes I ran with Alex, sometimes with both dogs, as Glenn, not surprisingly, had not taken Niki with him when he moved out. She had been a part of his life with us, and that was a life he had left behind. We could tell she missed him, and the kids tried to give her extra affection and attention. But she was clearly a one-person dog, and my heart ached for her.

During my self-indulgent days on the couch, a couple of good friends showed up at my door one day and insisted I "come outside and play." I was unshowered, dressed in sweats, with no make-up on. They pronounced me "perfect" for the day's activity, forced me into sneakers, then took me away from the house and up to Mt. Baldy, the closest (and tallest) peak in the San Gabriel mountain range. It was February, but with several inches of snow on the ground, the air was soft and warm and infused with all the intoxicating scents of the forest. We walked and talked for hours, the guys sharing with me their own divorce experiences, listening patiently as I verbally spewed about mine. The day marked a turning point for me. I realized I just needed to keep putting one foot in front of the other, focusing on my kids as I had after my first divorce, allowing the beauty of life to sustain me as I healed.

As part of that healing process, I enrolled in a graduate program to work toward my master's degree in literature, thrusting myself right back into long crazy days of working full time and attending classes at night. But I needed my hours to be filled with something other than self-condemnation, feelings of failure and, if I'm honest, loneliness. I found myself back in school, loving education, and channeling a wellspring of creativity. I wrote poem after poem about my life, my loves, my joys, my fears. I began to fill my journals with entries that had to do with the stuff of daily living, not with the shadow of regrets.

In the summer of 1994, I turned forty. I had just finished my third year of teaching freshman English at the high school, and I loved it. I had been to the beach several times with my kids that summer, and I was tan and fit, feeling healthy and alive.

That's when I found a new mole on my leg. A flat, black, suspicious looking mole. I can still remember the cold veil of gloom that drifted down over me as I sat in the bathtub, looking at it. This is bad, I thought.

And my next thought was this: Not now. Not yet. I had one more class to finish in order to fulfill the requirements for my master's. This was no time to be dealing with a disease.

This is honestly what my thinking was at the time, and it is indicative of my constant state, back then, of single-minded intensity. I had to finish that class to get that master's to get a few steps higher on the pay scale to provide more completely for my children before it was too late, before they had grown up and gone off to provide for themselves.

I did make an appointment to see my doctor—for the day after my final exam in that last grad class.

I wore shorts to my appointment so he could easily see the mole behind my knee. He walked into the exam room and, without even greeting me, pointed at my leg and said, "That's coming off today."

The first biopsy came back as positive for malignant melanoma. While my doctor was as gentle and reassuring as he could possibly be (you know it's bad news when your normally non-demonstrative doctor sits down beside you and takes your hand in his before he speaks), I knew enough about melanoma to know that if the biopsy were accurate, I may have only a short time left to live.

A second surgery—to remove a large chunk of my leg—was scheduled immediately, and another biopsy would be performed on the excised tissue. Waiting was an interesting proposition. When you're told you have cancer, a continuous loop goes through your head. It sounds something like:

I have cancer. I may die soon. I'm not ready yet. I have cancer. I can fight this. I may not beat this. I may die soon. I'm not ready yet.

And you just can't stop it. The year before, a good friend and colleague had been diagnosed with testicular cancer. The prognosis wasn't good. When he returned to work—barely alive, but alive, damn it—after chemotherapy that nearly killed him but saved his life, he told me about the surreal moments when you realize that life is continuing to go forward all around you while you watch, knowing that you're dying. He said, "A supermarket clerk would look up and smile and say, 'How are you today?' in a cheery voice, and I wanted to reply, 'I'm dying.'" He never did. His words came back to me when I experienced the same situation.

For the three days leading up to the surgery, I mostly stayed at home, sitting on the end of the couch, the same place I'd been so many afternoons after Glenn left. Nothing seemed important or worthwhile.

On one of those days, I sat slumped over with my head in one hand, the other hand hanging over the side of the couch. I don't know if I'd dozed off or had been in so deep a reverie that I wasn't conscious of what was happening around me, but I suddenly realized that my right hand rested on top of something very warm and furry. Alex, at some point, had come to sit beside me. His body rested against the side of the couch as he sat quietly, content to simply be there for me. I crawled down onto the floor with him, and he stretched out beside me, rolling over on his back.

As I stroked his belly, I recounted time after time that I'd been sad in the years since he'd come to be with us, and he had positioned himself close by, lying at my feet or leaning against my knees. I'd been so self-absorbed for so long, I had forgotten for a time how instinctive it is in a good dog to render aid. I'd been overlooking a tremendous resource for comfort in my life.

Alex and I had a long talk that day. As one will make promises to God in times of dire need, I promised him that if I survived this thing, I would endeavor to pay closer attention to him in the future, to never take him and what he meant in my life for granted again. Mostly he replied with heavy sighs. But I think he knew I was sincere.

For three days after the surgery I hobbled around, waiting for the second biopsy results. Finally, I called my doctor's office, ready to face my doom, to put my affairs in order.

The verdict was basal cell carcinoma, an easily treatable cancer. No melanoma. No death sentence. I would live to receive my graduate degree, to watch my children graduate from high school, perhaps college, and to spend more time with my dog.

Cancer changes everything.

The night I received my good news, the kids broke the toilet. I heard a loud crash, and when I called down the hallway to find out what had happened, no one would answer me. When I reflected upon it later, I realized how much I had hounded them over the years about not wasting money, not breaking things we could not afford to replace. They were afraid to tell me that one of them had knocked off the lid to the tank, breaking it in half. Finally Shali, always the brave one, came forward with the truth. And they waited, cringing. The old Mom, the pre-cancer Mom, would have ranted and scolded, admonishing them to be more careful. I asked if everyone was all right, if anyone had been hurt or cut by the sharp porcelain. No one had.

"Then we're fine," I said. "No one has cancer. Nothing else matters." It became my constant mantra for a very long time.

And I kept my promise to Alex.

Once my leg healed and I could walk without pain, we often went out early in the morning on the weekends before anyone was up and wandered the neighborhood. Alex loved these walks. I wasn't up to running yet, and it wasn't his style to walk sedately beside me while I trudged along, so I let him off the leash. He would run ahead and sniff every tree, every yard, then trot back to check on me, then run ahead again. I noticed everything, as people who have survived a life-threatening incident will do. The leaves on the trees were turning yellow, just like they always did in autumn, but being there to see the turning meant being around to see all the changes in life.

And suddenly, life was changing faster than I could keep up with it.

CHAPTER TEN

Shali, who had graduated two years before and had been working and going to school, was expecting my first grandchild in October—another reason (as if I needed one) for me to be around awhile longer. Ezra, Joanna and Sam were all struggling to get through high school unscathed, and I'd had my hands full trying to help them along as best as any distracted, imperfect single parent could. Shali's pregnancy had somehow catalyzed us, knit us together in a tighter bond, and we were all looking forward to the big event.

And, after ten years in the rental house, we were moving. Shali and Ezra had both taken economics classes in high school. When they learned how much more sense it makes to own a home rather than rent (in a normal economy), they began to gently urge me to buy a house. I told them repeatedly that I was a single woman with a short work history who would never qualify for a loan and had zero down payment; they simply countered my arguments by doing more research. One day Shali handed me the phone number of a real estate agent. Turns out I qualified for a government program which enabled people like myself to bid on repossessed, bank-owned homes. I needed no down payment, just a few thousand dollars to pay the closing costs, which I borrowed from my mom. When I realized I was going to live for a few more years, I began looking for a new home in earnest.

My grandson, Ben, a big strapping lad, was born on October 23, 1994. Several weeks later, I found the perfect home in Rancho Cucamonga. It had three bedrooms, two baths, a large kitchen plus a custom family room with a fireplace, and a large backyard for the dogs. Joanna graduated and moved out, and Shali moved in with Matt, Ben's father. (They planned to marry the next year if, my daughter told me, they could navigate the deep and dangerous waters of parenting together.) The new home afforded more than enough room for me and the boys.

On a rainy day in December, two days before Christmas, we packed up far more than we had arrived with ten years before, and we moved into the new house. The night before, Alex and I made sure our new home was safe for the family.

Although the property was in a great neighborhood, it had been vacant for over a year. Someone had bought it with the idea of fixing it up, but he'd run out of money and simply walked away, giving it back to the bank. While the corporate folks were working their way through the paperwork, unscrupulous members of the neighborhood (and having lived there now, I think I could point to which ones) had decided to help themselves to items left behind after the foreclosure. Items such as the bathtub faucet. And a ceiling fan from the dining room. And the garbage disposal from under the kitchen sink. They even stole the air conditioning unit out of the side yard. My new neighbors had already let me know that they'd frequently seen teens sneaking into the house at night.

But I was so thrilled at being able to own my own home that I could not contain myself. I really can't explain it; I just wanted to sleep in the house when it was still vacant, before it was filled with furniture, boys and noise. The day before moving day, I took my bed over to the new house and set it up. That night, I left Niki to watch over the boys, and Alex and I drove out to the new property.

I left the back sliding door open so that Alex could go in and out from the yard to the house. While I took a long hot bath, he alternated between trotting around in the empty rooms, sniffing every corner to trotting outside to pee on every shrub. Finally, I closed and locked all the doors, and we settled in for the night.

I should point out here that Alex was never really an aggressive dog, but in the few short years after I'd adopted him, he did make it clear to everyone that his job was to protect me, and he took his job quite seriously. The skateboarder who had ridden by so raucously the first day after Alex had come home to us, causing him to bark in defense of his yard, had been a particular nemesis for my poor dog—until he received what he had coming to him. For some reason, he enjoyed making Alex run along the fence and bark. In fact, if Alex didn't chase him, he would grab the chain link as he rode by, shaking it and making threatening noises. This went on for months, until the day I happened to be in the garage with my trusty dog at my side. The garage door was open and Alex was sitting sedately, watching the world go by, when suddenly we both heard the skateboarder coming down the sidewalk. Before I could get my fingers on Alex's collar, he was off, charging like an underwater torpedo, silent... but deadly. The poor skateboarder had no warning. One minute he was sailing past the house, cigarette dangling from his fingertips, the next minute my dog's teeth were clamped in the butt of his jeans. He didn't fall, but he did make an unflattering dismount from the board, dropping the cigarette in the grass. Alex had taken one bite and let go, coming back to my side as I called him. The angry boy glared at me.

"Your dog just bit me!" he shouted.

"Maybe if you wouldn't torment him every day, he wouldn't feel compelled to protect us from you. And aren't you a bit young to be smoking?" He was all of fourteen, if that. Still grumbling, he collected his board and rode off, as I continued to admonish him that if he persisted in bothering my dog, I couldn't be responsible for what happened when the dog was off leash in the front yard. The boy's mother showed up on my doorstep an hour later. She was a gentle but harried woman, and she wanted to know if Alex had had all his shots. I assured her that he had, and explained why my dog had felt compelled to bite her son. She agreed that he had gotten what he deserved, and let us know that, beyond a bruise and a scratch, he was fine, though his dignity was sorely wounded. I didn't mention the cigarette. He never bothered Alex again. In fact, he stopped riding past the house altogether.

Most of the time, Alex was a big shaggy loveable puppy. But some instinct clicked on in him the second he felt his mistress—the lady who had rescued him from dog jail, as I liked to remind him—was threatened.

I slept lightly that first night in the new house, dozing but listening at the same time. Around midnight, I woke to an eerie sounding whistle in the back yard. I thought at first I'd dreamt it, but when I climbed out of bed and stood by the window, I realized it was coming from mere inches away. The whistler was standing at the corner of the house, signaling to someone else. Alex followed me down the hall, the hair along his back bristling. Silently I unlocked the slider. I looked down to see Alex on full alert, ready to lunge out the door as soon as I pulled it open. I slid it open as quietly as I could.

"Go get 'em, Alex," I told him. He shot like a bullet across the yard, turning at the corner to chase someone along the side of the house. I raced to the front door and out around the side of the house, arriving in time to meet Alex, trotting back toward me from the neighbor's yard. The side yard gate hung open. I closed it carefully, then hugged my big furry protector who was now dancing around on his toes, wagging his tail and trying to get me to play with him. I wondered at his capacity to morph from stealth defender back into playful puppy mode so swiftly. But it is in the nature of dogs to live in the moment, responding to a threat when necessary, but moving forward to the next good experience in life as soon as possible.

On Christmas Eve, I left the house early and spent the day shopping for gifts for all of my children and my new grandson. On my way home in the late afternoon, I stopped at a Christmas tree lot and convinced the proprietor to sell me a large tree for twenty bucks. "Look," I said, pulling the cash from my wallet, "it's all the money I have left. And my kids need a Christmas tree." He took the money, loaded the tree into my truck, and I drove home to hurriedly get it in the house and in a stand, then make lasagna before Shali and Matt came over with Ben.

Our first Christmas Eve in the new house with the new baby created one of those enduring memories that families will recount decades later. In part, it was memorable because we were all together, safe and healthy. Mostly we remember it as The Christmas Eve When the Tree Fell on Nana. I had thrown the tree onto the tree stand with such haste that it wasn't properly anchored. At some point while we were all sitting around on the family room floor, opening gifts and laughing joyously, the huge tree suddenly fell over, pinning me beneath it. I could hear Shali frantically telling her husband to "get the tree off my mom!" and I could hear Ezra asking anxiously if I was okay. But for the life of me, I couldn't speak, I was laughing so hard. We had our first fire in the fireplace that night, my daughter likes to remind me, but I had forgotten to open the flue before I started the fire, so by the time Shali and Matt arrived, the house was filled with smoke, and poor Matt was conscripted to stick his head up the chimney and thrust it open. At some point much later in the evening, after having been rescued from the tree, I stretched out on the couch with my grandson lying on my chest and fell asleep.

I woke early to light rain falling on Christmas morning. Throwing on some jeans and a hooded jacket, I took Alex out to explore our neighborhood for the first time. We walked around the housing tract, misty sprinkles accumulating on Alex's fur, looking for all the world like tiny diamonds displayed on black velvet. He didn't seem to notice as he trotted ahead, sniffing each yard to learn who lived there, then returning to me to check on my progress. As we turned a corner, I saw Christmas lights blinking in the gloomy, overcast dawn, the yard filled with glowing animated decorations. Christmas lights were a simple pleasure we had been unable to afford for years. I vowed that by next year, even if we had to start small, we would have at least a string or two of lights to celebrate the holiday season.

What I had wanted for my children all their lives was a sense of permanence and stability, the opportunity to feel secure. In buying this house, moving away from the memories I had shared with Glenn, I felt we were all making a fresh start. A friend once told me, though, that "life is a series of problems to be solved." We faced many problems in the ensuing years, some quite easy to solve, others more complex and life-changing. In the end, I was to learn that immuring my children in a place I thought safe was not enough to shelter them from the dangers of the outside world. Sometimes we can try to do all the right things, make all the right choices, and bad things still happen.

Shortly after we moved into the new house, I came home from work one afternoon to find that Niki had been sick all over the family room. In recent days, she had been listless and lethargic, and I had brushed it off, telling myself that she was simply adjusting to the new place. But she had been slowing down for some time. We had all attributed it to her sadness in missing Glenn, though I sometimes wondered if something more was going on with her. Both dogs had annual check-ups and vaccinations; no matter how tightly stretched the budget was, it was something I had always insisted on. And since Niki had continued to eat normally, showing no signs of illness, I hadn't thought it necessary to take her to the vet.

Now I looked around the room at pools of loose feces soaking into the carpet and wondered what could possibly be wrong with her. And then I made one of those horrible errors in judgment that can haunt us for a lifetime. I called Glenn.

I have no doubt now that I called him because I was angry about his abandonment of Niki. It was if I projected my own scenario with Glenn onto the situation; it made me furious that after all of her devotion to him he could just walk away from her. When I called, I explained to him that I had depleted all my resources in buying the house and that I needed him to step up and help out with Niki's care. She had been a great companion to him, and it was only right that he honor her by taking her to the vet and being with her through whatever examinations and tests she had to endure at the hands of strangers. He told me he understood and would take her in first thing in the morning. I made arrangements to leave a key for him as I would be at work.

There was something ominous about coming home the next day when I was greeted by Alex alone. It was past four o'clock in the afternoon, and Glenn had said he would pick up Niki in the morning. The red light on the answering machine was blinking. I pushed play, heard nothing for several long moments, then Glenn identifying himself in a voice choked with emotion. His words were few and interspersed with long seconds of silence during which he tried to collect himself. He'd had Niki euthanized. I don't know why. I never learned what was wrong with her. In broken phrases he said something about the diagnosis and what the vet said, but I stopped listening once I knew she was gone. He may have had good reason. But a thousand times I have wished that he had waited to talk to me, ten thousand times I have wished I had taken her myself.

I had to tell the kids that night, and our joy at being in the new house was occluded by the veil of mourning. What a great dog she was. Though she had companioned herself with Glenn, we knew she loved us, too, and she had been part of our lives for almost ten years, from the time my kids were in elementary school until they were young adults. Alex seemed confused at first, looking for her in the yard and even in my closet (which she had commandeered as soon as we settled in), and I was touched as I saw the boys reach out to him, giving him extra affection in the same way they had done with Niki when Glenn left her behind. Eventually he adjusted to being an only dog. I considered getting another dog to keep him company during the day, but I loved my partnership with Alex, and I wanted to give him one hundred percent of my attention. He didn't seem to need another dog, just me. And lord knows I needed him.

I gave myself time to recover from Glenn's departure, immersing myself in graduate school, my job, my children. And then I attempted to begin dating again. Nothing ever worked out. Below is a paragraph from a journal entry I wrote in 1994 after hearing a lecture by Sam Keen, author of *Fire in the Belly*:

It seems that for two years I have invested time, energy, hope and dreams in finding that certain special man to share my life with. I have strayed off onto strange paths, only to have to stop abruptly and turn back, most times leaving someone wounded behind. It is time for me to come back to the main path in my life and to stay on it, no matter what that means in terms of singleness or celibacy or aloneness. I would rather be alone than hurt anyone again. I have things to do before I leave here forever. If a partner joins me on the road as I travel, so be it. If not, I will endure.

Keen had made the point during his talk that each of us has an individual path to travel, and that path should be the focus of our lives. We are fortunate if, while we travel that path, a partner joins us. But in order to remain authentic to ourselves, we must pursue our calling, using the gifts we've been given.

I tried to remind myself of this wisdom on a daily basis, but as my boys grew up and became busy with their own lives, it became harder and harder to be alone. I spent many a weekend morning hiking with Alex along the streams in Mt. Baldy, reflecting on what it meant to be an authentic person, to concentrate on expressing my gift rather than searching for a partner.

From another journal entry:

My palms are scraped. Alex just swam across a deep pool, so he is clean now, but I am covered from head to foot with dirt, as is my backpack. I have dirt in my eyes and in my shoes. Alex and I had to slide down a hill.... But... this is how I escape from it all. This is my retreat when the days loom long and lonely if I stay home to wait for the phone to ring. As hard as it is sometimes, especially lately, I must remember who I am and where I am going. The glass is half full, whether I can see it or not. One foot in front of the other. Alex is shaking water all over the page; it's time to go.

Hiking alone might have been a scary proposition without Alex beside me. I needed those long walks in the forest, and he was always there, moving ahead on the trail to scout for danger, returning often to check on my progress, and then heading out again, repeating the pattern a hundred times. When other hikers approached, I would step off the trail to let them pass, and Alex would stand in front of me, leaning into my knees, watching intently, displaying no aggression but clearly guarding me nonetheless. It was not a behavior I had taught him. He was following his natural instinct—his own gift, as it were, which served as an example to me. Alex never wasted time in self-indulgent questioning of how he should be ordering his days. He simply gave himself over to his innate canine inclinations.

When the passing hikers were fifty yards or so past us, my "Let's go!" signaled Alex's release from duty, and I would feel the tension melt from his body. In the next second, he'd be flying up the trail again.

What would I have done without him? Every afternoon when I returned from work, I was greeted by Alex's nose, pushing its way into the first crack of the opening door, his muzzle finding my extended hand before his eyes could even see me. He moved from room to room with me, was never farther than a few feet away. At night, he slept on the floor next to the bed. Oddly, he could be convinced on occasion to jump up on the bed and lie next to me for a nap—but only in daylight. If night had fallen, no amount of coaxing or pleading would get him on the bed. He would sigh heavily, head between his paws, considering himself, I suppose, on guard duty for the night—with one exception. On rare occasions, I would be out late with family or gone to some event. If I came home long past bedtime, Alex would jump onto the bed and lie beside me, whimpering and wagging his tail, as if he had despaired of my safe return. Eventually, when I was sleeping peacefully, he would jump back down to the floor.

It was through Alex that I learned how incredibly observant dogs are. As much as I wanted to, I couldn't hike every weekend; there simply wasn't enough time to do so with all the other chores I needed to accomplish on my days off. But somehow, on the mornings I intended to hike, Alex knew. And he would be ecstatic, running back and forth through the house, sliding to a stop in the bedroom doorway as I tried to get ready, looking at me with those comical brown eyebrows as high as they could go in expectant delight, then dashing off again. How did he know? Why didn't he act this way when I was getting dressed to go to work or preparing to go grocery shopping? How the heck could he tell that my intention was to go hiking? It took me years to figure out that he was keying on my selection of shoes. I was watching him one day as he lay on the floor in the bedroom, head on paws, recording my every movement in that mysterious doggie brain of his.

"How do you know what I'm planning to do?" I asked him. He hadn't reacted yet. But as I reached into the closet to grab my hiking shoes, I saw his head come up. He watched, waiting to see which shoes I would withdraw. I was incredulous. Could this really be the tip-off? I pulled the only pair of hiking shoes I had from the closet and held them up for him to see. He leapt to his feet, and the celebratory laps up and down the hallway began. Son of a gun.

I wish now I had taken him for a thousand more walks in the forest. It is the only guilt I feel about my time with him. He took such good care of me and asked for so little. Walking in the woods made him over-the-moon happy, and he deserved that happiness every day. In grad school, after studying Peter Meinke's untitled poem written to his son, Peter, I wrote a pastiche of it:

This is a poem to my dog Alex
whom I have walked a thousand times
though not often enough, I know,
and not at all lately—for want of time,
not for want of affection.
I have seen your eager ears, tail wagging,
appreciated your need to run free in
those woods that smell of strange, exotic wild things,
have heard your sighs in the evening when
you know another day is closing without escape
from
the yard and the small confines of the house.
I think you know that you are a good dog,
as I have told you and retold you a thousand times
because you guard my fragile frame,
because not once in a decade have you failed
to greet me at the door,
nor ever once turned away from my call, and

because no matter how deep in the well of sadness
I have fallen, I can still see your eyes,
waiting patiently for me to surface.

Those brown eyes are what I remember most about
Alex Haley, those eyes that were always watching,
always waiting for walks or ear scratches or chew toys
or naps together. His eyes and his willingness to protect me no matter what.

CHAPTER ELEVEN

Shali did marry Matt after they had been together for some time. Unfortunately, their marriage didn't last past the first year. When they separated, she came to stay with me while she went back to school, realizing, just as I had some dozen years before, that she would need an education in order to support her son.

I loved having her back home again, especially since she brought with her my delightfully happy two-year-old grandson. She was working and doing well at school, making progress toward her degree, until she was somewhat derailed by a tall dark handsome man. I didn't like him from the moment I met him. Dustin was sullen, moody, taciturn and wholly lacking in respect or consideration for those older than himself. He represented that "every parent's worse nightmare" scenario of the brooding, black-clad, tattooed musician who writes incomprehensible lyrics, screams them into a microphone and is willing to sacrifice anyone and anything to see his band become successful. My daughter fell for him as only a young woman can for a melancholy outsider on the fringe of society who only needs the softening love of a woman to redeem him, bring him back from the edge of despair.

I didn't mind that she had found romance after her struggles with Matt, nor did I mind watching Ben in the evenings so that she could spend time with him. Shali has always been a bright, pragmatic person; I assumed that with time she would come to see this unhappy soul as the self-centered, self-indulgent guy he was. Unfortunately, she did not come to this conclusion soon enough.

One day after work, Sam shared with me that he had heard Shali and Dustin arguing outside his window when Dustin had brought her home after a date. This pleased me, as I assumed Dustin's boot to the curb was imminent. When I responded with a light-hearted "Good!" Sam became angry and agitated, telling me I had no idea what had been going on. That's when I tuned in. What he'd heard Dustin say was this: "Don't you understand? I don't want to hit you. But you make me do it." I couldn't believe that he would stand outside on my front porch and threaten my daughter. I found it even harder to believe that Shali would allow it to happen. At five foot two inches and a hundred pounds, she was the smallest of my children, but she was also a tough woman to contend with. I wondered what was going on.

"Make her stop seeing him," Sam demanded.

What my son didn't know as he pleaded with me to intervene was that just before I'd left the house that morning I'd gone looking for my blow dryer in Shali's bathroom. She hadn't even tried to hide the Early Pregnancy Test kit; the box was right there in the trash can.

I could think of little else that afternoon and evening. Just my daughter. My beautiful, laughing daughter, our resident dreamer, the gentlest of my children, who cupped spiders in her hands when she found them in the house and relocated them outside. This same happy young woman had become, in eight weeks, withdrawn, morose and secretive about her relationship with this sinister man. How does one bring up the elephant in the room without causing further estrangement?

"Sweetie, what's going on with you and Dustin?" I asked the question as soon as she arrived home, while we were putting groceries away together. I might as well have said, "Shali, I demand that you stop seeing that wretched young man." It would have had the same effect. In minutes we were arguing, both voices louder than they needed to be, and somewhere in the accusatory exchange I threw in, "And was the result of that pregnancy test positive or negative?" So much for tender, maternal sensitivity.

She glared at me, then shot back, "Negative, if it's any of your business," as she fled the kitchen.

"It is if you're living with me and I'm supporting you," I called to her retreating back. Stupid, stupid things we say....

For several days, she hardly spoke to me. I felt paralyzed. What is the correct course of action here? Confront her again, alienate her further, driving her closer to him? Or ignore the situation and hope to God that he doesn't hurt her too badly before she comes to her senses? I didn't know what to do, so I did nothing.

Two weeks after our heated conversation, I was thrown out of my inertia by a shock wave when my daughter showed up at my workplace after being beaten by him.

Until that day, I had always appreciated the glass and steel construction of my classroom door. I could look through it and see far out into the field which bordered the east side of the campus. It was lovely. But on that day, as I was in the middle of a lecture, I looked up to see my daughter's battered face through the window in the door. She was crying, both arms wrapped around Ben, who straddled her hip. Yes, my grandson was with her and had seen his mother being hit in the head with a baseball bat. That was the first thing she told me as I stepped outside.

She was sobbing, overwrought with emotion, recounting how Dustin had threatened her, chased her, hit her, and finally picked up a baseball bat, telling her he was going to kill her. I heard every word she said while at the same time clearly, lucidly thinking, 'This is my little girl. This is my tiny precious baby girl. Who would do this to her? She has always been one of the kindest, most generous and compassionate people I know. How could someone ever do violence to her beautiful face, her beautiful soul?'

And yet my mind was keenly focused on what my daughter was telling me, how she managed to get out of Dustin's house, and had only kept him from chasing her by tossing his car keys into his car and locking them in. She'd driven straight to me for help.

"Mom, when he gets his keys out, he'll go to your house looking for me. He knows how to get in." Here is one of the dangers of bringing the stranger into the house. He had learned at some point that I always left the back door unlocked for my son who could never keep a house key more than a few days. Worse, he had already become acquainted with Alex, my beloved bodyguard. He 'knew' Dustin now and would let him in the house.

"And he's probably carrying his gun. He has a nine millimeter Glock that he takes with him wherever he goes." I don't know why I was surprised by this. I wasn't at her next words.

"And he's high, Mom."

When I asked what drugs he'd been taking, she shrugged her shoulders and said simply, "He takes anything he can get his hands on."

I'll admit, I shouldn't have left work and gone to my house that day. Common sense would dictate that, given the circumstances, the wise thing to do would be to call the police from a remote location and have them deal with the situation. I was in shock. I wasn't thinking clearly. No, that's not true. My thoughts were clear and to the point: I just wanted the opportunity to hurt him in some way.

I deposited my daughter and my grandson in a safe place, then turned my truck toward home, twenty minutes away. With my cell phone, I calmly called the Rancho Cucamonga police department, explaining that there was a man in my house, that he probably had a gun, that he had assaulted my daughter, and that he was under the influence of drugs and alcohol. I expected, given the gravity of the situation and the length of time I had to drive, that police officers would be waiting for me when I arrived home. They were not.

In fact, the neighborhood was quiet and serene as I rolled slowly down my street. I began to hope that the police had already been there, that the demon had been exorcised. I pulled into the driveway and got out of the truck quickly. Dustin must have been watching from the window. He immediately emerged from the house.

I can recall the moment vividly. He came down the walkway toward me and what I keyed on was his shirt. He was wearing a white T-shirt with some sort of design or insignia in red splashed across the front.

That's when it happened. The split second shift from the person I had been in the morning to the person I would forever know myself to be henceforward. More than anything at that moment I just wanted to feel a gun in my hand. I wanted to lift my arm and calmly squeeze back the trigger and feel the recoil and smell the powder and watch his white T-shirt slowly soaking up his blood until he was lifeless on my front lawn. The image of it didn't shock or sicken me. It comforted me.

The truth is, I didn't own a gun, have never allowed guns in my house—even now. My dad was a cop and a hunter, so I grew up around handguns and rifles and shotguns. But having guns in a house with children is asking for trouble. In high school, I saw the hole that was blown in the thigh of my best friend's little brother when he set a rifle between his legs to clean it. When I became single, a good friend offered to help me get a small handgun to keep in the house. "No, no way, not ever," is the gist of what I told him. Good thing. If I'd had one that day, I know I would have used it.

In seconds, as his cold, dead eyes glared at me and mine were riveted on his shirt, I thought:

I could kill him.

I would kill him.

I do not own a gun and that is the only factor that keeps me from killing him.

If I killed him and went to prison, how bad could it be?

If I were inside the house and he broke in and I shot him, the law says I may do so without penalty as long as I can demonstrate that he was inside before I killed him and that I feared for my life.

Each notion slid swiftly across my mind in the time it took for me to step onto the lawn and make a wide arc around him toward the door.

"What's wrong?" he asked, in the most gentle, non-menacing tone I'd ever heard him use.

"You know what's wrong," I told him quietly. "The police are on their way here. You need to leave." With that, I stepped into the house and closed the front door. My hand was still turning the deadbolt when his fist hit the door. He began pounding and shouting.

"What's wrong? What did I do? Why won't you talk to me? Where's Shali? I want to see Shali!"

Alex was there at the door to greet me, and stepping around his wagging tail slowed me down as I hurried to get to the back door. I had noticed when I'd driven up that the side gate was wide open. Now I saw that the sliding glass door was open as well. I pulled it shut just as Dustin came around the corner into the backyard, headed toward me. He started pounding on the glass with his fist. As I walked away, he moved to the kitchen window. The last thing I glimpsed before I ducked into the hall was Dustin sliding the window open a few inches, as far as the lock would allow, then sticking his enraged face through the open space and screaming.

"I want to see Shali! I didn't do anything! She's pregnant with my child!"

He pounded his fist on the window again and again, and I marveled that it didn't break.

Grabbing the phone in the den, I dialed 9-1-1. My dialogue with the dispatcher was surreal. She was matter-of-fact, almost bored in her tone. I tried to emulate her calm demeanor, though I sensed Dustin's drug-induced desperation, and I feared for my life. As we conversed, I could hear him outside, charging from window to window, trying to find one that wasn't locked, pounding on every one he came to, bellowing at the top of his lungs, demanding that I let him in.

"Is the man at your residence now?" the dispatcher asked after I told her I'd called the police over twenty minutes ago. Apparently she couldn't hear him screaming.

"Yes, he's trying to break into my house," I answered.

As we talked, I placed myself in a hallway, away from any windows so that he couldn't see me. At first

I stood, my back against the wall, but when I realized my legs were shaking, I slid down to the floor. Alex, confused and anxious but ever vigilant, sat on the floor leaning into me, eyes, ears and nose alert to every change in the direction of the bizarre sounds outside. True to his courageous, loving persona, he kept moving his body between me and the origin of the possible threat.

We were waiting now, the dog, the dispatcher and I, for men with guns and bulletproof vests to show up. Those moments were long... enough time to consider a number of what ifs.... What if Dustin did manage to break a window or a door and gain entry to the house? I wondered for a moment if I should find a weapon and hide somewhere. With no little irony, I realized there was a baseball bat right there in the closet at my back. Could I hit him hard enough to knock him out, get behind him somehow and aim for his brain stem? Would it kill him? But no. As soon as I considered it, I knew that if I had to, I would run for the front door and try to get out before he found me. This was not about self-preservation. It had more to do with my diverging thoughts. What would become of my daughter if her boyfriend shot her mom? If one day she had to explain to the child she was carrying that her father had killed her grandmother? Conversely, if I somehow found a weapon and killed him in self-defense, how would I explain to my grandchild that I had killed her father? These were my thoughts while Dustin continued his pounding and ranting and I continued to answer all of the dispatcher's questions in a falsely calm tone.

("How tall is he, ma'am? How much does he weigh? How old is he? Do you know his address and telephone number?") I also had to consider what would happen to Alex if I tried to confront Dustin. I had no doubt that if Dustin came toward me in a menacing way, he would have to go through Alex to get to me. Dustin knew this, too, as he had been made aware of Alex's protective behavior when he first started coming to the house. If anything were to happen to Alex in all of this, it would devastate me. Just as he stood between me and danger, committed to keeping me safe, I had to act in a way that would keep him safe as well. Having him there meant the world to me, and I tried to calm myself by stroking his head as he leaned into me.

In the midst of it all, Alex suddenly stood, his eyes focused at the end of the hallway. There was a door there, leading into the garage. It had a deadbolt, but we never locked it.

I approached the door cautiously, ready to bolt in the opposite direction if Dustin came through it into the house, but then felt some relief when I heard him pounding on another door, the entry door from the side yard into the garage. That one I knew for certain was locked. I flicked the deadbolt on the door in front of me, locking it, just as I heard a loud commotion of wood splintering and hardware screeching in the garage. Seconds later the doorknob in front of me moved back and forth as Dustin tried to open it. I would discover later that he had torn the smaller door completely off its hinges with his bare hands in order to get into the garage.

The police finally arrived, forty-five minutes after my original call. The dispatcher told me they had arrived, and I moved to the front window. They pulled into the driveway, and I watched as Dustin strolled out of the backyard, suddenly sedate, approaching them casually as if he'd just been doing a bit of gardening out back.

I'd like to describe how the cops grabbed him and threw him to the ground, handcuffed him and pushed him into the back of their car, how I sat with my daughter in court as he was charged with attempted murder.

None of that happened, of course.

As Dustin and the two officers seemed to be chatting amiably, I joined them outside to see what would transpire. Although he was eventually arrested on a charge of assault with a deadly weapon, the officers didn't think he'd really done much to get arrested for, since the bludgeoning of my daughter had occurred a few miles away in a neighboring city.

"It's not our jurisdiction," they told me. "You'll have to go over there and file a complaint."

They didn't find a weapon on him and they didn't care that he was under the influence since he was walking (having parked the car he stole from his grandmother a block away), and they certainly weren't interested in anything he'd done while he was on my property that day. I ended up just telling him to leave and that my daughter would never see him again. At that point, he suddenly collapsed in the driveway and began moaning almost incoherently, threatening to kill himself. I told him I thought doing so would be in everyone's best interest, at which point the police officers reprimanded me sharply, commanding me to go back inside my house. From the window, I watched Dustin casually stroll off down the sidewalk a few minutes later.

I want to say that after that day, Shali cut all ties with Dustin, but she didn't. At first, she believed whatever lies he told her, that he'd never hurt her again, never do drugs, whatever. She told me she had to maintain contact with him because, after all, they would be raising a child together. In the last trimester of her pregnancy, she moved in with him and remained there until several months after the birth of my beautiful granddaughter, Hali, attempting to make a family out of the chaos of that young man's life. Not until the night he held a gun to her head and threatened to kill her did she leave him for good.

The day Dustin hurt my daughter, my only thought—my instinctive thought—was to do whatever it took to keep him from hurting her again, whatever it took to protect those I love. I know that Alex's instincts were exactly the same. The truth is that despite the tough guy image of his Rottie and Chow ancestry, he was terrified of loud noises. A car backfiring would set him trembling, and the pop and whistle of fireworks on the Fourth of July would send him fleeing into the darkest corner of my closet where he would remain, shaking like a leaf, panting in severe anxiety, until he felt safe again. Yet on that day, no amount of Dustin's pounding on the doors or windows could send him fleeing to the closet. And I am absolutely certain that if Dustin had entered the house, Alex would have done whatever he could do to keep me from being hurt.

In the days and weeks that followed that ugly incident, I thanked Alex incessantly for being with me, being my bodyguard, and I walked him often just to make sure he knew how much I appreciated him.

On one sunny spring day, I put on my hikers and was surprised to see Alex express only half-hearted excitement at the prospect of going for a walk. He didn't do well in the heat, and I thought it might be warmer than I had anticipated or that perhaps I'd been walking him so much lately I'd finally drained off his excess energy. We got as far as the empty field across the street before he collapsed in the dirt.

I don't remember how I got him home. He weighed 70 pounds, and I've never been a very muscular person. But I somehow lifted and supported him to get him back home, then one of the boys helped me get him into the car. After we moved to Rancho Cucamonga, I continued taking the dogs to Dr. Chung in Chino Hills as he was an excellent vet. I called the office to let them know I was coming. Then I drove like a madwoman all the way there.

Dr. Chung drew some blood, and I sat on the floor of the exam room, holding Alex's head in my lap, waiting for the results, my hands shaking and heart pounding.

"This is very disturbing," the vet said upon returning to the room. "It looks like he's been poisoned."

Poisoned. Something... Someone... had poisoned my dog. My best friend.

"Can you save him?" I could barely ask the question. Alex remained on the floor, panting heavily. I thought for a moment I would have to make a decision about ending his suffering, and I didn't think I could hold it together.

"Maybe." Dr. Chung's single word gave me enough hope to begin breathing again. He explained that there had been damage to the liver, but that the degradation might be arrested with medication. I was prepared to have Alex hospitalized, and I told Dr. Chung I wanted the best treatment available, regardless of the cost. He sent me home with a bottle of pills and instructions to keep Alex quiet and make sure he had plenty of fresh water.

I spent the remainder of the day in my bedroom, mostly sitting on the floor with my boon companion, stroking his fur, brushing him, willing him to recover.

The next day, he seemed a bit better. He was up and around, eating and drinking. I vacillated between hope and despair, wondering if I were simply seeing what I wanted to see. Days went by. He had not yet been restored to his usual happy, dancing self, but he seemed no worse. I allowed myself to relax, though only a little, and went to spend the evening at the home of a man I had recently been dating. I was still there when my pager went off, a 9-1-1 message from Ezra.

"Something's wrong with Alex," he said when I called. From his tone, I knew the situation was dire and that he wasn't telling me everything. Tony had picked me up, and he drove as fast as he dared to get me home, while all I could do was sit and stare out the window of his truck, trying not to break down.

I had feared the worst and the worst was what met me at home. Alex had crawled from my room to Ezra's, seeking help, I suppose. He still lay sprawled on the floor, his body already stiffening in death.

Through everything I had endured with my children—my first divorce, the second, my cancer—they had rarely seen me shed so much as a tear. A rigid stoicism had set in during my years with Art and while the birth of my first child had softened me somewhat, allowing me to shed tears on occasion, I had become adept at suppressing my emotions, convinced that giving rein to them only exemplified weakness.

But the moment I knew Alex was gone, something inside me broke open and there was no stopping the tears.

Tony, helpless beside me, attempted to offer comfort in the form of "Don't cry, baby, there's nothing you could have done," which only deepened my sobs. The one thing I could have done for Alex was to be there with him, to hold him as he passed. I felt I had failed him. It only made the wound deeper.

Eventually Tony gave up and left me alone with my dog, going next door to borrow a shovel. Some time later, paralyzed with grief, I watched Tony and Sam gently lay Alex's body in the grave they had dug. I sat beside him, my body wracked with sobs, stroking his fur one last time. I couldn't watch as they covered him with earth.

Ten years. He had watched over me for ten years. For an entire decade, I had slept with his body sprawled on the floor beside my bed, heard his contented sighs in my dreams. He had run with me, hiked with me, cuddled for naps and greeted me nose-first every day for nearly one fourth of my life. I felt safe as long as Alex was beside me. I could not imagine my life without him.

Ellie, Ian, Osa

CHAPTER TWELVE

In *Shaggy Muses*, a book which chronicles the lives of famous literary women and their dogs, Maureen Adams describes the relationship between Emily Bronte and her formidable yet devoted mastiff, Keeper: "While she was writing Wuthering Heights, Emily relied on Keeper to be her anchor to reality." For the ten years that Alex had been with me, my life had been in a state of flux. I had been married and divorced, had seen my daughter married and divorced, had graduated college—twice—had begun my career as a teacher, had endured what concluded as a minor bout with cancer and had welcomed two grandchildren into the world. Through every tempestuous storm and halcyon moment of that decade, he was *my* anchor, the one constant source of love and affection I could depend on.

Without him, I was adrift.

Hiking had always been my escape. When the hectic routine of parenting, teaching and maintaining a household single-handedly became overwhelming, I would drive to Mt. Baldy or the foothills with Alex and walk until he was happily tired and I had generated enough endorphins to feel good again. After he was gone, I didn't hike for months. When I finally did, every step carried me deeper into a dark, lonely place in my mind. Hiking alone, I felt less safe, and I was conscious of the solitary person I had become. I didn't hike again for a long time.

A year passed in which I alternated between thinking I would never find another dog like Alex and chastising myself for being unwilling to open my heart and home to another shelter dog. When finally I felt I was ready, there followed a period of mistakes and missteps as one dog or another either didn't fit into the family or was heartbreakingly lost.

The first was a yellow lab puppy. I brought her home from a cage in a pet store because I couldn't stand to see her there. She was sweet and adorable—and she peed whenever she became excited, which was every time anyone spoke to her. I don't know what I was thinking; I had no time to work with a puppy. I had begun teaching for Chaffey Community College several nights a week to augment the household income, so I was gone a lot. I quickly realized that, unlike an older dog who is content to wait patiently in the yard or the house until someone comes home, this little fur ball needed someone with her most of the time. I found a young couple with a small child who fell in love with her the minute they all laid eyes on her. They scooped her up and took her home to be their son's first dog.

A few months later, I tried again. I stopped by the same pet store and this time they had two Dalmatian pups in the same cage they'd kept the lab puppy in.

But these girls were older, about five months. There was no room in that cage for them to play or stretch their legs, and they whimpered at the door, desperate to get out. I bought them both from the despicable pet shop owner who hedged when I tried to ask her where the pups had come from. Knowing what I know now about puppy mills, I'm sure that's where she was getting her inventory.

I named them Maggie and Emily. It took them twenty-four hours to destroy my backyard, chewing everything from plant stalks to patio furniture. Separated, they were calm and submissive. Together, they were the hounds from hell. I found a family with kids to shower Emily with the attention and affection she deserved, then began to work with Maggie. Slowly, as the weeks fell away, she became more calm, and even more slowly but steadily, I began to bond with her. When I had just reached the point where I had begun to look forward to walking with her around the neighborhood every day after work, I came home one afternoon to find the backyard gate pushed open and Maggie gone. This was not something she could have accomplished herself. I have no doubt that someone took her, probably someone who had seen her walking nicely by my side. She was a beautiful dog. I never saw her again.

And then there was Mykel, the purebred black Lab I bought from a breeder, driving all the way to Central California to pick him up. He was a perfect example of Labrador confirmation and temperament, a gorgeous dog with a sweet, loving disposition. And he was crazy. Though I worked with him every day, teaching him basic commands, walking him, running him, his activity level was so high he was nearly uncontrollable. Inside, he was a frenetic ball of energy that had to be watched constantly. Outside, he jumped incessantly at the back slider, begging to be allowed back in. I worked with him for months, trying to get him to calm down, but to no avail. As each day passed, he became larger and stronger, and I became more anxious and stressed about his behavior. One of my students who owned horses and other livestock offered to take him so that he would have a half acre of land on which to run and play with her two dogs. When I tearfully dropped him off, he made friends in a matter of seconds with the other dogs, then took off around the yard, running and playing tag with them. It seemed the perfect solution. Two weeks later I received a call asking me to come and get him because the family had been unable to stop him from chasing their sheep. Ultimately, Mykel was handed over to a Lab rescue group who understood his need for long periods of strenuous exercise and would find a suitable home for him.

I'm sure my loss equaled a gain of great love and companionship for the family who took Mykel on, but I knew I had failed him, and I was angry with myself for a long, long time because of it. Had I been able to draw upon the wisdom of Cesar Milan, the "dog whisperer," at that time, I know I could have learned the skills I lacked to be a good pack leader for Mykel. But Cesar had yet to come onto the scene, changing the way we all interact with our dogs, and the advice I continued to receive from fellow dog lovers proved ineffectual in curbing Mykel's exuberance, no matter how many hours I played with him or ran with him.

After a year of attempting to work through his issues, it broke my heart to give him up, and afterward I was simply defeated, my heart aching again for a dog that was lost to me.

Back in 1990, the year that Glenn had taken his leave of us, Shali had given me a homely little black kitten for my thirty-seventh birthday, proclaiming proudly that she had chosen the runt of the litter, the kitten least likely to be adopted. Ah, my daughter knew me well. The tiny mewling thing grew to be a haughty yet affectionate friend, and I named her Calpurnia after the housekeeper in *To Kill a Mockingbird*. Cal and Alex were never best friends, but they had eventually come to accept each other's presence, each, I'm sure, out of his or her own sense of *noblesse oblige*. Cal always slept on my bed, and Her Majesty would occasionally deign to allow Alex to join us for a nap. If he crawled too close, she would swat him on the nose, a harsh reminder to keep his distance. He could have broken her neck with one snap of his jaws. Instead, he would lower his big head onto his paws with a deep sigh, looking at me with eyes that begged me to see what he was willing to tolerate out of his devotion to me.

Once Alex was gone, Calpurnia was thrilled to be the spoiled only child, to take possession of the entire house as her domain... until one rainy afternoon in early spring of 1997.

I was in my classroom during lunch when a student walked in holding the warm poncho she should have been wearing. Wrapped in its folds was a tiny black kitten. The poor thing's eyes widened in terror as I lifted the heavy fabric and peered inside.

"Hey, Boo," I said, quoting Scout Finch. I didn't mean to name him, but it stuck. Nicole had wanted to keep him, having faced down the bullies who were trying to stone him to death near the horse corrals on campus. But when her mother flatly refused to take in one more stray animal, Nicole came to beg me to take him, tears running down her face as she cradled the little feral kitten in her arms. How could I refuse?

He was so weak when I took him home, I didn't expect him to live long. He spent the weekend huddled under my bed, creeping out at night to eat and use the shallow litter box I had set up for him in my bathroom.

The following Monday after work, I took him to my new vet, Dr. Olmstead, a jovial woman who poked him, prodded him, pronounced him "lovely" and proclaimed that he would grow up to be a beautiful cat. Surprisingly, he did just that.

It took Cal months to adapt to the presence of the little upstart Boo, but eventually she came to accept his company on "our" bed. He was always intimidated by her, though he grew to be three times her size. I loved them both dearly and was grateful always for their companionship, but I was still without a bodyguard or hiking partner. In addition, it became clear as Boo grew up that he was terrified of dogs. Several attempts at adopting rescue dogs were thwarted when, upon first sight of the big black kitty, they chased him through the house and into the safe haven of his bedroom closet. One dog actually dove in after him, knocking the closet door off its runners, and I fear would have hurt him had I not been there to intervene. Most dogs will ignore a cat if the cat refuses to back down to them. But even the best dogs will engage in the chase if a cat—or rabbit or squirrel—runs from them. I had quickly become deeply attached to Boo and wanted to protect him from any more traumatizing events, so, for a while, I just stopped looking for another dog.

In 2000, my brother Dan made the decision to move from the Los Angeles area to the state of Washington. Dan was the one who'd brought his dog Manfred into the church for our sister's vocal recital. On his journey through life, he'd always had a dog as his closest companion. For the previous twenty years, that dog had been Black Bart, a large dog of unidentifiable ancestry who had been my brother's sidekick in countless adventures. Dan also had a big brown furry dog named Ellie Mae. He had raised her from a pup to be a companion to Bart, though she was half his age.

Dan would be staying with friends in the Seattle area, embarking on a new career, and he knew he couldn't take the dogs with him. He had waited to leave, in fact, until he was ready to say good-by to Bart, who was now so old that he was deaf, nearly blind and crippled with arthritis. My brother, as brave as he was heart-broken, took his beloved dog up into the hills of San Fernando where they'd spent so much time together and tearfully gave him the injection that would relieve him of his pain forever.

He took Ellie to stay with Mom, who was now retired and living in a mobile home park in Victorville, a small town in the desert, eighty-five miles east of Los Angeles. Dan's reasoning was that Ellie would be a companion and protection for our mother, who lived alone, and if things fell through with his new job, he would return to California and take her back to live with him.

At first, Mom was happy to have Ellie's company. And Ellie was a great watch dog. Every month or so I'd drive up to visit, to see if Mom needed any odd jobs done. Ellie would bark at me until I came close, and then she would finally recognize me, wag her tail and greet me enthusiastically. Mom lived on a cul-de-sac, beyond which sprawled several acres of desert land. She took Ellie for daily walks, letting her off the leash when they reached the open spaces so she could chase rabbits. (She never hurt them. I saw her catch one once, and she looked as surprised as the rabbit was terrified. She held it gently in her mouth for a moment, then dropped it, watching it run for cover but making no move to catch it again.)

After awhile, Mom's mobility began to decline, and she found it difficult to accomplish the daily walks. So she would load Ellie into her car, drive to the end of the road, then let her out to run in the desert. After half an hour or so, she would call her back and take her home. Eventually, even those outings were curtailed, so every time I went up to see Mom, my visit began with a long walk for Ellie. There was no yard to speak of at Mom's place, just a fenced enclosure around the mobile home and patio, with gravel and cement as a ground cover. Ellie was an older dog, but still pretty lively. She quickly learned to recognize my truck, and her excitement at the prospect of getting out of the yard could not be calmed until she'd had her chance to run free, chase a few rabbits and sniff every new scent in the desert.

Even as a mature dog, Ellie never grew out of her puppyhood. Part German Shepherd, part Chow Chow, she was a round fuzzy girl with floppy ears and a sweet disposition. It wasn't long before I found myself heading up to the desert more often, just to spend time with her. I loved to see her joy as she trotted around exploring the open spaces. It was healing for me.

Most times I would head to Mom's early on a Saturday morning so I could walk Ellie in advance of the desert's stifling heat. One day, due to a late start, I didn't arrive at Mom's until almost noon. I found Ellie sprawled on her side on the cement next to the porch steps. Mom's outside thermometer showed one hundred degrees. When I stepped inside, I began to call Ellie to come with me, until Mom shouted from the living room for me to leave her outside. When I asked her why, she said that she'd decided Ellie would be an outside dog from now on. Repeated queries on my part just resulted in terse responses, offering no further explanation.

Since my teen years and all that transpired with my wicked step-father, my relationship with my mother had remained on rocky ground. I loved her, and I'd forgiven her for those times, but Mom continued to display resentment toward me for various reasons, and that resentment had deepened after I'd gone back to school. Mom, with her eighth grade education, felt intimidated by anyone with a college degree, including her own daughter. Occasionally, she would snap at me if she felt I was being condescending, which was never the case. But perception is everything.

That day, I knew enough to drop the subject. But I couldn't stop thinking about Ellie. My brother was a free spirit who had always lived life on his own terms, but he had always considered his dogs family members. He never married, and as my sister observed once, his dogs were his children. When I got home that day, I called Dan. We talked for a long time about Mom's diminishing ability to care for Ellie. Dan defended her, even when I told him Ellie had been banished to the outdoors. He argued that Mom had seemed lonely in recent years, and I countered that keeping Ellie outside all the time and never walking her didn't allow her much of an opportunity to be a companion. Dan stubbornly refused to see a problem. I hung up even more disturbed than I had been before I called.

Over the next few weeks, I visited Mom often. Each time I went up, it seemed that Ellie's health had declined a bit more. I told myself I was probably just imagining it, that I was projecting my own issues of emotional abandonment by my mother onto the dog. Perhaps it was the summer heat, I tried to convince myself, that had slowed Ellie down as we rambled in the desert.

Every time I returned from my mother's I would vent to Shali. After her final separation from Dustin, she had moved back in with me, where I was blessed to have my grandchildren at hand every day to spoil and adore, tucking them safely into their beds at night. They generated light, warmth and joy in my life where there had been little for some years, and every day when I left work, I looked forward to seeing them at home.

Shali had gone back to school, but she was also working part time at a local vet's office. We talked at length about Ellie's situation and my concern for her. Finally one day my sensible daughter sighed in sympathetic exasperation and said, "Mom, just bring her home." She was right.

I called my mother and told her I wanted to bring Ellie home to live with me the following weekend. She didn't agree, and she said we'd talk about it when I came up there. She sounded annoyed, and I knew that she would call Dan, but I was resolute in my intention and willing to risk alienating both of them. It wouldn't be the first time.

On Sunday, when I arrived at Mom's, Ellie greeted me with her usual unrestrained joy, wagging her tail, licking my hand, ready for her walk. I bent over to pat her back and saw that she'd been chewing at her side. She had a thick undercoat, inherited from her Chow ancestors, which required a lot of grooming. I searched through her thick fuzz to see if she'd picked up a tick, but found nothing, just clumps of matted, slobbery hair. I sighed and went in to face my mother.

Our battle of wills was brief but intense.

"I called your brother," she snapped as I walked in the door. "He's not happy with you."

"Mom."

I wanted to say so much to her. I wanted to tell her that throughout my life, my brother had rarely been "happy" with me, because he was the privileged oldest child, my mother's admitted favorite, and our sibling rivalry had been fierce because I refused to acknowledge him as being superior to me. While she chose to patronize him, I demanded he respect me as an equal, something he only began to do later in our lives. I knew he would be angry with me if I took Ellie, but he was a thousand miles away. Let him be angry. My first priority was the welfare of the dog.

"Mom," I said again, my tone as calm as I could force it to be. "Ellie is a good dog. She deserves to be happy and well cared for. If there's one thing I know, it's that dogs want to be wherever their humans are, not shut outside in the heat or the cold. You don't want to let her in, and you haven't been brushing her, and you can't walk her anymore. You know I will walk her and brush her. And at my house, she will be inside and part of the family." I stared at her intently, defiantly, and as her eyes met mine, something shifted between us. We'd had this conversation before, decades before. But that was back when I was fifteen and powerless to be the advocate Rufus needed. The anger I had felt then simmered still, just below the surface, and I have no doubt she could see it clearly in my eyes. Back then, I had been unable to protect the dog I loved. Not so now. "I'm taking her home with me, Mom."

After a brief pause, my mother rose from her chair, went to the kitchen and began silently collecting Ellie's things in a bag. I don't think she was angry with me. She acquiesced because she knew I was right. It just hurt her pride to admit it. And she owed it to me. She had never apologized for anything I'd gone through in those awful years with Art, and out of deference to her as my only parent, I never spoke of that time. As a parent myself now, I understood how we live with guilt, though we may never admit it to our children, may never find the right moment to apologize for the mistakes we've made. In a small way, in giving me Ellie, she was trying to make up for what happened with Ruf.

And so I offered to do some chores for my very human and somewhat frail mother. Then I took Ellie Mae—now Ellie Mae Murphy—for one last walk in the desert, brought her back, and loaded her into my truck for the long drive home.

Ellie's homecoming was monumental. It began with her first foray onto grass in over two years.

I kept her on the leash as I led her through the house and out the slider into the backyard, then let her go and stood back to watch, with Shali, Ben and Hali alongside to welcome her home as well. She sniffed, peed, then flopped over on her back, paws in the air, wiggling back and forth as her huge fan of a tail swept the grass. As we watched, I pointed out to Shali where Ellie had been biting at her side. She offered to take her in to work with her the next day to have her checked out by the vet.

Ellie was content to sleep on the floor of my bedroom that night, though Boo and Calpurnia were not happy that she was there. I told her that under no circumstances could she chase these kitties, and while she did appear disappointed at that news, she obeyed without incident, and the cats soon felt safe around her. (Calpurnia, from time to time, felt compelled to inflict a haughty swipe across poor Ellie's nose, just as she had done to Alex on occasion. I never ceased to be amazed at her courage in standing up to a creature ten times her size. Her ferocity was without measure.)

On Monday, I headed off to work with Shali's promise that Ellie would go to the vet's office with her. I came straight home that afternoon, hoping for some time to walk Ellie before dinner. But she wasn't there. I called Shali at work, and she let me know that she'd be a bit late getting home—but Ellie wouldn't be coming home with her.

"She's going to stay the night," she told me. "She's having surgery in a little while."

Ellie had a foxtail lodged deep in her ear, a broken tooth and a live deerfly larvae growing under her skin. That's why she'd been biting at her side, and as my strong and stoic daughter described how "creeped out" she was when the vet made her hold her fingers over the spot until she felt the larvae moving, my heart went out to this gentle giant of a dog who had somehow maintained her good nature despite what must have been a hellacious toothache, an earache, and a worm wiggling beneath her skin.

Shali stayed through Ellie's surgery and made sure she was comfortable for the night, then came home, bringing the deerfly larvae in a small jar. It was the size of a small caterpillar. Poor Ellie Mae.

Dan called that night, furious with me for taking 'his dog.' Hearing she had just had surgery made him switch gears a bit. When I recounted her inventory of medical issues, he finally agreed that bringing her to my place was the right thing to do.

"She's a good dog," he said, his voice cracking. I knew that he felt guilty for leaving her behind, and I tried to reassure him that she would have a great life with us, and that we would take good care of her until he could return for her, or until the end of her life.

I think because I made this promise to Dan, it kept me from fully bonding with Ellie. I loved her dearly, but I continued to think of her as "Dan's dog," and I think I subconsciously tried to keep from being too attached because of the real possibility that he might someday return to claim her. And while Ellie clearly loved and trusted me, she was the kind of great family dog that returns everyone's affection. Ben and Hali loved their big furry new companion, and she was great with them.

But within a few short days, I noticed further issues with her which needed to be addressed.

I asked Shali one morning if the puddles I kept finding on the kitchen floor were emanating from her small children or Ellie Mae, though I was pretty certain I already knew the answer.

This time I took Ellie to Dr. Olmstead. Due to her age and other contributing factors, Ellie was incontinent. She wasn't intentionally wetting the floor, she was just having a tough time controlling her bladder. I suddenly understood why Mom had banished her from the house, and I think she didn't want to explain why because she knew I would insist on taking Ellie to the vet immediately.

Dr. Olmstead put Ellie on a daily medication (phenylpropanolamine) which the ever-voracious dog cheerfully gulped down in chunks of canned dog food, and in no time we were no longer walking through puddles in our socks.

The bigger issue I discussed with the vet that day was Ellie's arthritis. She had trouble getting up when she'd been lying down, and her back legs seemed stiff. Dr. Olmstead confirmed my diagnosis, and I was immediately crestfallen.

"So I should limit her activity?" I suggested. I didn't want to make her hike with me if it meant inflicting pain on her.

"To the contrary," Dr. Olmstead replied, "the more she walks, the more limber and pain-free she'll be."

And so overnight my daily routine was altered dramatically, which led to many unexpected adventures, some harrowing and some miraculous.

The next morning after I'd had a cup of tea and skimmed the local newspaper, I put on my sneakers and clipped on Ellie's leash. It was only 5:00a.m. and still dark outside, but sufficient light glowed from the street lights to illuminate our way, so off we went. Ellie, cheerful as always, gave herself over as only a dog can to exploring the origin of every scent on our neighborhood parkway. I held her on a retractable lead, so while I kept up a steady pace, she still had ample opportunity to stop and sniff as she made her way along behind me.

I found myself enjoying that pre-dawn time. I thought about my plans for the day, made a mental list of things to do, then ruminated on some writing ideas. Ordinarily at that time I would be heading to the gym after that initial cup of tea, but I had decided I would alter my work-out somewhat to accommodate the time to walk Ellie. I was determined to walk her every day, mostly because of what Dr. O. had said. But also to honor Alex. The one regret I had after I lost him was not walking him as often as he deserved—which was every day. I wanted to make whatever life Ellie had left a good one, to make sure she had everything she needed.

That first morning, we did a fifteen minute walk. The next day, we went a little farther. By the end of the first week, she would start prancing the minute I threw my legs over the side of the bed in the morning. I stopped reading the paper first and didn't get my cup of tea until we returned, which had us out of the house by shortly after 4:00a.m. most days. The walks woke me up, warmed me up, and I was still getting to the gym by 5:00, ready to jump on the treadmill and coax out the endorphins and serotonin I needed to help me stay on an even keel.

I loved this time in my life, and frankly, I was a bit spoiled. I started my day with a quiet walk with Ellie, heading off to the gym afterward, then went from there to my job teaching high school (which I loved). I often came home exhausted but eager to spend time playing with my grandchildren. To top it off, Shali would usually make dinner, and she is a fabulous cook. In the evenings I would read or sing to Ben and Hali as they snuggled into their beds, and then I quickly headed for mine.

Of course, life is never absolutely one hundred percent perfect.

CHAPTER THIRTEEN

Because they shared a child together, Shali had continued to be in contact with Dustin. He rarely came by the house; I think at some point she had shared with him that I was more than willing to risk life imprisonment if it meant the opportunity to mete out justice where justice was deserved. But she would sometimes take the kids to spend time with him at his grandmother's house in nearby Upland, attempting, I suppose, to at least give him the chance to be a father. Not surprisingly, he made little effort to bond with his daughter. He lacked any part of that skill set.

Shali knew how strong my feelings were about the other fifty percent of Hali's DNA, so she never elaborated much on her time spent with him. But one day she approached me with the news that Dustin's grandmother had died and other relatives were casting him out of the property which had been inherited elsewhere. He would be moving into an apartment—and could not take his dog, Ian. Her plea, "Can we bring him here?" was followed by a dozen or so promises in rapid succession: She would pay for his food, license and vet bills; she would pick up after him and Ellie in the backyard; he was used to being outside in all weather, and she would keep him in the backyard if that's what I preferred. And so on. Ben, already an animal lover at his young age, loved Ian, she told me, and would be heartbroken if Dustin relinquished the dog to a shelter. And it might be temporary, she said. If Dustin found a better living arrangement, he might be able to take him back.

She'd had me at, "He's an older dog but no one gives him any attention anymore—they just keep him in the backyard," and I'd made up my mind for certain when she'd said that Ben loved him. But I didn't tell her that.

"Is he housebroken?"

She answered honestly that she didn't know, as he was always outside.

"Well, I guess we'll find out."

Ian's coming to live with us was on two conditions. If it didn't work out—if he chased my cats or didn't get along with Ellie or showed any sign of aggression toward the kids, she would have to work hard to find a suitable home for him. And once we took him in, Dustin lost all claim to him. The county dog license would be in my name, but Ian would be Ben's dog, and Ben would not have to live under the threat that his dog might be taken away from him at some possible point in the future.

All parties agreed—young Ben most joyously—and several days later I came home to find poor Ian on the patio, curled up on an old blanket by the back slider. He was a crazy quilt mix of breeds, part German Shepherd, part terrier, part who-knows-what, though Ben,

I'm sure, would like to believe he was part wolf. He did have wolf-like coloring to his fur, a mottling of brown, black, gray and white. His eyes definitely had a lupine quality, with the cold stare of a wild animal forced into captivity.

Ian's current physical condition angered me, and I stood fuming on the other side of the glass door watching him as he got up and walked stiffly around the patio. He was over-weight and had thick calluses on his elbows from sleeping on concrete. Everything about his demeanor, from his tucked tail to his drooping ears, indicated a depressed dog.

Shali hadn't introduced him to Ellie as she had been waiting for me to be present. I had her take Ian away from the door, then I simply let Ellie out to make her own introductions. After a bit of tail sniffing, my happy girl invited the new boy to a romp around the yard, but he simply stared at her. We brought out some of Ellie's toys, including a tennis ball, and threw them around, trying to engage Ian in some sort of play. His disinterest spoke volumes. Shali admitted she had never seen him play, and she wondered aloud if he'd been played with as a puppy.

"I don't think he knows how to play," she concluded.

Impossible, I thought. But it was true. Even when he had settled in with the family, he never really learned how to chase a ball or give himself over to frolicking with Ellie, though we did eventually find some things he liked to chew... too many things.... Once we determined he behaved well in the house, he slept in the kids' room at night, next to Ben's bed. In the morning it was not unusual to hear Shali swearing or, on occasion, Ben crying, because Ian had chewed something to bits in the night—crayons, toys, books— anything with Ben's scent. He had definitely recognized Ben as his pack leader. Ian was a grumpy old codger, but I liked him because he loved Ben, and there is something about the bond between a boy and his dog that is both primal and sacred. He followed Ben around the house or out into the yard or wherever Ben happened to go. Most endearing was this dog's insistence on lying sprawled beside the tub while Ben took a bath.

"Ian, seriously," I would hear Shali tell him, "I won't let him drown."

Countless times, Ian was unintentionally splashed with water and more than a few times Ben decorated his poor dog's head with bubbles, but his stoic companion never complained, just stuck by his boy as if it were his life's purpose to guard him.

At first, Shali made attempts to walk Ian. But the kids, understandably, insisted on going, so it became an awkward family outing, all four trying to shuffle down the sidewalk together while Ian first dragged them forward, then stopped abruptly to pee, halting the parade. Shali was all about sharing and allowed both kids a chance to hold the leash. But Hali was small and Ian was strong. More often than not, he pulled the leash from her tiny hand, and if Ben or Shali didn't immediately grab it, they would spend the next twenty or thirty minutes trying to chase down their errant dog. Even now my grandchildren delight in hearing me tell the story of their mother running around the neighborhood muttering "goddamn it, Ian," as she made repeated but unsuccessful attempts to secure the end of his leash.

And so it evolved that I began taking Ian on my early morning walks with Ellie.

The first attempt was disastrous, as the two dogs were incessantly crossing and tangling the leashes. But I quickly discovered that if I walked at a faster pace and stayed just ahead of them, they would trot on either side to keep up, and we moved along much more smoothly that way.

We observed change in Ian that was both rapid and dramatic. He slimmed down to a healthier weight. His coat became soft and lustrous. And it wasn't long before the stiffness that had made him seem old and decrepit had melted away. We walked every morning, and Ian Dog loved it. And, I felt, he deserved it for watching over Ben so carefully. If I had gone to a shelter looking for a dog, Ian would not have made my short list of possible adoptees, but every day that I saw him with Ben, I was grateful that we had taken him in.

And then we took in another.

Our annual tradition for Thanksgiving involves heading up to the desert to have dinner with my brother and his family. Kevin and his wife were in a state of transition that autumn; their children had grown up and left home, for the most part, and they had purchased a piece of property in Spring Valley

Lake, a beautiful planned community in Victorville where they were having a home built. This was an exciting time for them, and over dinner they shared stories about working with the architect and details of the blueprint that had been created to their specifications.

After dinner, I chatted with my nephew, Paul, about basketball, the Lakers and Kobe. While we talked, I noticed my brother's dog, Osa, making her way unobtrusively among the guests, sliding along the wall behind chairs and human legs. At one point, she gently rubbed against Paul's leg, and he kicked her away with his foot without so much as a pause in the conversation.

Osa was a beautiful dog, part Sheltie, part Shepherd, as Sapo had been, with a long, graceful muzzle and deep golden eyes. My brother loved to hunt, and he had raised her from a pup with the idea of having a dog to flush water fowl and perform other hunting dog duties. But she had become the family pet. Now in her senior years, she was mostly ignored, the invisible family dog, ever-present but rarely seen.

I waited for a lull in my conversation with Paul, then called to her. She crept up timidly. Her long hair was matted and hung from her sides in large clumps. She smelled bad, like she hadn't been bathed in a long, long time.

My sister-in-law watched me petting her.

"Poor Osa," she sighed. "We've decided that if she doesn't die before the new house is ready, we're going to have her put down. No one pays attention to her anymore, and we don't want any dog hair in the new house." While her remark may sound callous or superficial, it had been generated from some tough quality-of-life conversations for both human and dog. Denise suffers from severe allergy and asthma issues, so critical at times that she has ended up in hospital emergency rooms, struggling to draw breath. For Kevin and Denise, the new house represented an opportunity to demonstrably limit the number of allergens in the household—bare floors, double-paned windows. . . and no pets. In their minds, Osa was at the end of a good life and had only a slow, painful decline to look forward to. But while I understood their necessary conclusion, I knew from my recent experience with Ellie and Ian what a bit of attention and affection—especially those daily walks—could do for an older dog.

I gave myself some days to think it over, then called Denise to ask if they would consider letting me take Osa. I knew they felt she was on her last legs, and Kevin explained that his vet had detected a heart murmur when Osa was a pup. "She was never supposed to live this long," he said. But I felt that even if she lived a short time with my family, she would be treated to daily walks, grooming, the company of other good dogs when the humans were away and of course, the regular and lavish doling out of affection by one small boy and one tiny girl.

Denise talked it over with Kevin, and they agreed. To this day, I can't thank them enough for their decision. When Osa came to me, my heart broke with hers, and when our hearts healed, they had somehow melded together.

Since I would be off work for two weeks around the Christmas holiday, we decided that winter break would be a good time to bring Osa to her new home. I offered to come get her, but Kevin insisted that they would bring her down.

Even if we could have foreseen the way in which Osa would be traumatized, I don't know that we would have done the exchange any differently. Some things in life are just achingly hard.

Anyone who has spent time being attentive to animal behavior knows that animals are capable of a wide range of emotions. To a non-believer, I might be dismissed as naïve or guilty of anthropomorphizing. But I would argue that I have observed dogs, cats and horses exhibit the entire spectrum of emotion from ecstatic joy to intense anger and everything in between, including empathy and confusion. True dog lovers know that dogs are capable of feeling love—deep, abiding, unconditional love.

So it was with Osa. She had been with my brother all her life. When he brought her into my home, she sat quietly, devotedly beside him. Later, as he walked to the door, she was beside him as well, assuming they'd be going home. I don't expect that she understood his words when he turned and said, "No, Osa, you stay here now," but his intention became clear to her as soon as he closed the door, walked to his truck and drove away. She was being left behind. I watched as she ran to the window, pushing her nose through the blinds to watch as his truck pulled away from the curb. She whined, trotting back to the front door and turning to me with pleading eyes, begging to be let out, and my heart broke for her. I went to her as she panted and whimpered and moved from door to window and back again. But she could not be comforted. Not in that moment and not for days afterward.

The first night, I had to clip a leash onto her collar and drag her to the backyard to relieve herself. Back inside, she went straight to the front window and looked out again. She would keep her vigil there for days, her chin resting on the sill until she slumped against the wall from exhaustion. For three days, she did not eat. I told Shali I feared that Osa would simply grieve herself to death and I would feel a fool for bringing her to such a miserable end.

"Mom," she said, in that same tone I used with my own mother, "give her time. She'll get over it."

On the fourth day, I coaxed her to eat a little by hand feeding her. On the fifth day, she ate a bit more.

I didn't walk her in the morning with the other dogs right away as I wanted to give her time to adjust. And while she remained steadfast near the front door, waiting for my brother to come back for her, she had not interacted with the other dogs at all, so I hadn't gotten any sense of how they would all get along.

Early on, I made an attempt to brush her, and the whole incident went so badly that I stopped, realizing I would have to gain her trust before I could touch her in that way. Where Ellie and even poor, neglected Ian had been happy to have the attention and gentle massage of a grooming, Osa stiffened and backed away, frightened and confused.

When she finally began eating and drinking regularly and—miraculously—moving away from the front door to come lie near us in the family room, I decided she was ready to join us on our morning walk. And walking her changed everything.

For the first block, I held all three leads, but quickly admitting the madness of that idea, I stopped and unclipped Ellie. "You stay with us," I admonished, pointing my finger in her face. I knew Ellie wouldn't take off—unless she saw a cat—and would follow right along with us, but I did see cars in the neighborhood at 4:00a.m., so I kept a close eye on her. I didn't want her dashing off after a kitty and getting run over.

With Osa on one side of me, Ian on the other and Ellie delighting in her new freedom to mark every neighbor's front lawn, we traveled a loop of several long blocks. My little trio of twelve-year-olds behaved like the settled, mature folks they were, and returned home to have their breakfast and then lie contentedly about the house. Well, perhaps Osa had not yet reached the point of being content, but she was visibly less anxious and more relaxed, and then more so with every passing day as we continued to walk each morning.

A year or so after Alex died, the land on Sixth Street behind my property had been developed into a small housing tract and community park. From time to time I had taken Ellie there just before dawn when the park was empty to let her run off leash. On New Year's Day, I decided to do the same with all three dogs.

I'd stayed up late with Shali and the kids on New Year's Eve, so I slept a bit later the next day. The sky was just beginning to lighten when I stepped outside with the dogs. They were confused at first when I pulled them away from our usual route, and I had to juggle all three leads as we crossed Sixth Street. But once we reached the other side, Ellie began to dance and whine. She knew what was in store. I unhooked her leash, and she bolted across the wide expanse of green lawn. Ian was next, and he took off after Ellie.

As I unclipped Osa's leash, I petted her head and looked into her eyes.

"You stay with me now, Osa. Please don't run off."

I will never forget the moment. She stood motionless at first, watching the other dogs who had reached the fence line that bordered the park on the far side and were sniffing their way through the young trees along the edge. She looked back at me for direction, so I gestured with my arm.

"Go on, go play."

And while her gentle lope was a far cry from the mad gallop of the other two, her body language told the story of an ears forward dog who is eager to explore a new world. For the first time in two weeks, she untucked her tail, wagging it tenuously as she headed off to join her comrades. I gave myself a moment to shed some tears of joy for her, then went about the task of cleaning up after them, plastic bags always at the ready.

Oftentimes, in processing through some challenge in life which requires growth or change on our part, our progress forward is made in very small steps—sometimes two steps forward and one step back. This held true for Osa as well. She had settled into our daily routine and looked forward eagerly now to our morning walks. But she still had a long way to go before she would recover from her emotional trauma.

The day after our breakthrough in the park, the holidays were over and I had to go back to work. The morning started with an early walk for the dogs, as usual, then I slipped out the door at 5:00 to head to the gym, then on to work. Shali and the kids were still sleeping when I left.

I returned home many hours later to find my daughter annoyed to say the least. She told me how she'd been awakened early by a dog's loud whining and barking. She'd hurried out of bed, assuming something must be terribly wrong, only to find Osa standing at the door where I'd left, wailing inconsolably.

"Mom, she was like a toddler who's been left behind at daycare."

Attempts to comfort her or cajole her with treats proved ineffective, and the racket went on for a good half hour before Osa finally went into my room and collapsed on the floor, surely convinced that she'd been left behind again.

While Shali related this sad tale, Osa stood close enough to lean her body against my legs. I bent down to pet her head and stroke her beautiful long nose.

"Don't worry," I told her, "I'll always come home." If only they understood everything we say.

She did not allow me out of her sight all evening. The next morning, as I walked out of the house and into the garage to leave for work, I heard her begin to whimper and howl on the other side of the door. At least Shali was already up.

Osa's separation anxiety went on for weeks. When I left each morning, she would sit by the door howling while Shali and the kids tried to ignore her as they got ready for school and work. When she heard the garage door roll up in the afternoon, her loud whining barks would begin in earnest again until I had made my way into the house and she could lean into my legs to reassure herself and, finally, calm down.

Eventually, the length of time she spent crying at the door gradually diminished, but it was several months before she could let me leave without reacting. She always followed me to the door, though, and she'd be there again when I returned, waiting to greet me with her cold nose, just as Alex had always done.

Once I knew for certain that Osa had no intention of running away from me, I let her follow on our walks off the leash. She was the slowest of the three dogs, and she trailed along on the parkway next to the sidewalk. I often had to slow down to allow her to catch up, which was fine with Ellie and Ian because it afforded them extra time for sniffing trees and shrubs and flowerbeds.

I ordered a heavy waterproof coat with a blanket lining from Lands End so that we could walk in any kind of weather, and we did—rain and wind and cold. My favorite, of course, were the summer days when I could don shorts, a tank top and flip flop sandals to walk them before sunrise.

We saw some amazing things on those walks. Sometimes, walking in the pre-dawn hours, I would see a garage door open, the overhead light on, a man bending over a car engine or working on some other project that had kept him up all night. Once, walking past a neighbor's darkened house on the other side of the street, I saw him framed in his living room window—stark naked—just gazing out into the night.

Our neighborhood was populated with a number of mockingbirds, each in his own territory, of course. I love these plucky bug catchers who will roust a cat away from an active nest or swoop down to intimidate even a large dog if it comes too close. Mockingbirds mimic the sounds they hear, from the cry of a kestrel to a telephone ring. And for years, when I lived there on Meadow Street, their colorful songs were what signaled the return of spring for me. Some time late in March, when the days were growing longer, I would hear in the twilight hours a mockingbird singing, and I knew that soon everything would begin to blossom and warm again. I would hear the mockingbirds singing as I drifted off to sleep at night, and when the dogs and I ventured out in the early hours, I heard them again, laying down their sweet, melodic trills upon the silence of the night.

One morning as we walked in early spring darkness, I heard what sounded like the excited chirping of sparrows. It couldn't be, I told myself, as it was still a good two hours before dawn. We followed the sound, and around a corner in a small tree on the parkway I could see birds jumping from branch to branch. In the light of a streetlight, I could see dozens of sparrows and finches flitting around. Their chatter was as loud as it would have been in broad daylight. I walked to within several feet of the tree, wondering if the birds had been alarmed by a cat or an opossum. But there was no sign of a predator. They were simply awake. It was such an odd thing to behold, and to this day I have no explanation for it. The event filled me with a sense of having been the recipient of an extraordinary gift, as if, while everyone else slept, I had been witness to a secret, behind-the-scenes performance of Nature. It heightened my consciousness, made me aware of what phenomenal scenes play out when the humans retreat and Nature has the world to herself.

One such scene, as I stepped out the front door into the darkness one morning, was chilling. In the street I saw the silhouette of a dog just in time to hold Ellie, Ian and Osa back, not yet unclipped from their leashes. We all watched as this shadow moved into the light from our streetlamp and resolved itself into a large coyote. Behind it were two more. They were taller than my dogs, but very thin. They had come marauding on this night, looking for food. The dogs beside me didn't stir, just watched as their wild cousins trotted silently around the corner, back toward the vineyard and the open fields beyond.

The 'yotes weren't the only danger we encountered in those hours of stealth and mayhem. In fact, were it not for these good dogs—Ian in particular—I am convinced that on one particular night, my life might have taken a disastrous turn.

A springtime event in the city of Upland is the annual Lemon Festival, a tradition begun many decades ago when the area below Mt. Baldy was planted with citrus orchards for as far as the eye could see. In the fall of 2002, I had left Jurupa Valley High School to teach at Upland High. The following spring, some of my students, a few of whom would be working at the various food venues, invited me to attend the festival. Still single after ten years, I often found things to do on the weekends that involved large crowds. I confess I enjoy strolling anonymously among strangers, observing human behavior and making mental notes for future writing projects.

On this particular day in late May, I enjoyed the music of some street musicians and browsed through the various vendor booths until late afternoon, then bought a funnel cake to eat as I ambled my way back to the truck. It had been a glorious, sun-drenched day, the type that compels one to indulge in snacks that are as memorable as they are unhealthy. I stood by my truck, finishing the last of the sugary pastry. And then I realized I was dusted with powdered sugar, down my shirt and covering both hands. In retrieving my keys, I smeared the stuff all over the pocket of my jeans, then on the door handle of the truck, then on the steering wheel. Laughing at the mess, I pulled away from the curb and drove the short four miles back to Rancho Cucamonga. I parked the truck in the garage but left the door up. The warm spring days had awakened the grass, and I'd considered, as I pulled into the driveway, how unkempt the front lawn looked. I would get the mower out and cut the grass as soon as I cleaned up the powdered sugar mess. I left my purse in the truck along with a courier bag I kept writing materials in. I would get to it all in a moment, as soon as I washed my hands. But the phone was ringing as I walked through the door into the house, and I rushed to answer it, gently pushing my way past Osa and Ellie who were there, as always to greet me. (Ian remained always with his children, if they were home.)

I don't remember who it was that called that day. I know I talked for a long time and then was excited to tell Shali, our family's elephant lover, about the pachyderm I'd seen at the festival. And then we got caught up on the events of the day, per our usual routine. So immersed was I in that beloved routine of dinner with Shali and the kids, sprinkled as generously with love and laughter as my funnel cake had been with sugar, I completely forgot about mowing the lawn, the mess in my truck and the garage door left wide and invitingly open.

The first thing I noticed when I stepped out the front door the next morning shortly after 4:00a.m. was the strong odor of cigarette smoke. So strong, in fact, that I stopped on the front porch to take a look around. We were not unaccustomed, the dogs and I, to watching cars drive slowly through the housing tract at that hour, an arm slung carelessly out the window, dangling a lit cigarette. And we'd encountered other people walking—one young man came straight up the middle of the street, talking loudly on his cell phone as if it were the middle of the day. Someone must have passed by recently, I decided, as Ian dragged me off the porch, always the bad boy who was never interested in what *I* wanted.

He pulled me down the path to the driveway, and that's when I stopped dead in my tracks again as I saw the gaping dark hole of the garage.

Stupid.

I'm sure I must have said it out loud. I suddenly remembered all my good intentions, and now I felt like a complete idiot as my absent-mindedness might have cost me a great deal of sorrow. I managed to drag Ian, who was straining to get to the sidewalk, far enough into the garage to look into the front seat. Crisis averted. All my things were piled just as I'd left them. I heaved a sigh of relief. Then I quietly tried to convince Ian he should follow me into the house so I could hit the button and close the roll-up door, but he was having none of it. He knew the routine called for us to spend the next twenty to forty minutes trotting down the sidewalk in search of scent and adventure, not walking out one door and back in another. He couldn't be coaxed, and he'd literally dug his heels in; I could hear the sound of his nails scraping the cement as I tried to tug him in what he perceived was the wrong direction.

"*Okay, okay,*" I whispered, slackening the leash just long enough for him to realize he'd gotten his way. He stretched it tight again as he pulled like a sled dog toward the sidewalk. I stopped him one more time, just long enough to unclip Ellie and Osa on the fly. I had decided in those few seconds that, with no one around, it would be safe to leave things as they were, run to the end of the block, then run back on the other side of the street. It would shorten our usual time out dramatically, but I didn't want to risk being any farther away. I took off at a run, all three dogs instantly matching my speed. Concealed in shadow was someone waiting for us to do just that.

It took me perhaps three minutes to reach the end of our block. I never slowed, just looked around for cars and made sure Ellie and Osa were at my heels as I crossed the street. The dogs were anxious and confused by our pace, but they stayed close, and we headed back toward home faster than we'd gone out.

When I neared the house and looked into the darkened garage, I could see, even from across the street, that the interior light in my truck was on, illuminating the cab. As we crossed over and the dogs trotted up the driveway, the light went out as the door clicked quietly closed.

Someone was still in the garage, standing, waiting. And there I was at the end of the driveway... standing... waiting. Ellie and Osa had moved away from me to sniff the lawn and wait by the front door to be let in, anticipating breakfast. Ian stood beside me, unmoving, waiting, too, to see what crazy thing I would ask of him next.

What to do.

I have mentioned that I am half Irish. I have plenty enough temper and stubbornness to prove this side of my heritage.

"Whoever is in my garage, you need to come out," I called into the dark. When there was no response, I repeated it with much greater volume and far less patience. I heard a shuffle, glimpsed movement in the darkness. The silhouette of a man emerged, a bag hanging from his shoulder. By his height and frame and gait, I thought he was Ricky, a friend of my son's who lived four houses down and had been caught before pilfering from homes in the neighborhood.

"It's just *you*?" I said with disdain.

"Yeah, it's just me," a deep male voice answered, one I'd never heard before. His tone was sarcastic, a dangerous edge to it.

He took a step in my direction and the security light over the garage clicked on. Instantly he raised the bag from his shoulder to hold it in front of his face. I understood; he didn't want to be identified.

Time slowed.

He moved the bag slightly to see where he was going as he advanced down the driveway toward the sidewalk. In that brief moment—two seconds, maybe three—I tried to take in as much information as I could: Late forties. Reddish brown hair. Black jeans. Dark jacket. He carried a heavy duty metal flashlight in his right hand. And I saw him glance at Ian. Ian-Dog, who did not care a wit for me, I'm sure, but stood steadily at my side, looking intense and wolven, his tail neither wagging nor tucked, just tense and still, his eyes riveted on the stranger.

The air nearly buzzed with the electricity of our thought processes as I contemplated the potential weapon in the man's right hand and he wondered, I'm sure, just how vicious the gray mongrel at my side might prove to be. I reached down and curled my fingers around Ian's collar, a bluff to make the man think I was holding the dog back.

A decision was made.

The man swerved in a wide berth around us but not so wide that I couldn't see now in the glow of the security light that the bag he held was my courier bag. Bulging from the top was my purse... with wallet, credit cards, checkbook and cell phone. *Stupid.*

As the man reached the sidewalk, he let the bag down, his back to us now. His step was casual, his stride even as he began to walk off, my personal property swinging from his shoulder.

Rage replaced reason.

"Are you going to give me my stuff?" I spoke as evenly as I could while advancing toward him, pulling Ian with me. He glanced back over his shoulder—not at me, but at the scary dog now right behind him.

"Sure." Defeated, he spat the word out like a flavorless wad of gum, lifted the bag from his shoulder and in one motion heaved it onto the front lawn, the contents splaying out in all directions.

He never slowed or quickened his pace, just kept going, a certain defiant swing to his thin hips, down the block, around the corner and out of sight.

When I saw him disappear, I became conscious of the adrenaline rush as my heart pounded in my ears. My hands shook wildly as I tried to quickly gather things from the dew-covered grass. He'd taken my CD's and the wet cases kept slipping from my trembling fingers. All the while as I shoved things back into the courier bag I kept up an inane babble directed at Ian. It had to do with what a good dog he was and a real hero and how he'd saved us just by being his grouchy old self, and I threw in what a stupid human I was, and I stopped two or three times to hug him, affection he disdained, as he just wanted to get inside and get his breakfast.

Less than sixty seconds after our burglar made his nonchalant escape, I was on the phone with a dispatcher from Rancho Cucamonga Police Department. Less than two minutes after that, a squad car screeched to a stop in front of the house. I was outside waiting for him. I gave him a description through the open window of his car, and he burned rubber pulling away from the curb. He returned ten minutes later. The perpetrator had vanished, of course.

Frustration edging his tone, the young officer warned me of a "recent parolee" who was living two blocks above our friendly neighborhood. He fit my description of "late forties, reddish brown hair." He was a drug addict and part of his lifestyle included burglary.

Only after the officer left and I went through my things did I realize the thief had pocketed my house keys. The remainder of that Sunday was spent changing the locks on every door. Everything else was accounted for, including all my CD's. What a fool. If he hadn't been so greedy, he could've gotten away with my purse from the front seat, cash, credit cards and all, but he had to go rooting through the console for Josh Groban, Diamond Rio and Joan Baez.

CHAPTER FOURTEEN

The next morning found me right back out there at 4:00a.m., of course, for how could I tell my good dogs we wouldn't be roaming the streets anymore? No, I refuse to give in to fear, so we headed out as usual, but I do confess I was loaded up with a large flashlight and my cell phone. These precautions lasted for only a few outings, however. After the cell phone dropped from my pocket into the wet grass when I ran with the dogs in the park one morning, and I had to go back and re-trace our trail with the flashlight to find it, I stopped carrying it. It was extemporaneous, anyway. I had my lungs. And three big dogs.

A few days after Ian and I faced down our burglar, I called Kevin and told him the story.

"I'm surprised you didn't sic Osa on him," he said. I thought he was kidding.

"Um, really?" was my skeptical response. I couldn't imagine my gentle, shy girl going after anyone. Little did I know.

The next weekend I stepped out the front door into the still dark Saturday morning, dogs in tow, to glimpse movement in the yard across the street. My house faced a corner house that fronted on the intersecting street, so I had a view over a low block wall into my neighbor's backyard. Someone was back there. I unclipped the girls' leashes and began to walk warily across the street, brave Ian by my side.

Suddenly three figures dressed in black burst from the shadows, running straight toward us across my neighbor's lawn, vaulting the fence and turning to run up the sidewalk toward the corner. All three were young males, teenagers.

"Get 'em, Osa!" was all it took. She bolted after them, barking and growling fiercely, her long body stretched to its length as she raced to catch them. They were fast, but she was faster, and I heard one of them scream—whether in fear or pain, I cannot say— as they tore out of sight around the corner.

I started to jog in that direction, but just as I did Osa returned, sniffing her unhurried way toward me. I hugged her and praised her. And laughed. I never would have imagined she could be so tough, and the discovery of this side of her endeared her to me all the more. When most folks meet me—the quiet bookworm who is wary of other humans—they draw the same conclusion I had with Osa: Pushover. But under the right circumstances, I have a tough side, too.

"We're fearless," I told her, kissing the top of her head. "Or stupid."

For the second time in a handful of days, I hurried the dogs inside so I could grab my phone and call Rancho Cucamonga P.D. An officer responded quickly. He woke my neighbor, and the two of them walked back to inspect the yard. They found a shed door wide

242

open but nothing taken. Once again, we had foiled the thieves. My neighbor, a soft-spoken Vietnamese man who knew only the barest of English phrases, thanked me profusely, and I just as profusely apologized; it must have been terrifying to be awakened from sleep by a man banging loudly on his door and identifying himself as the police. Later that afternoon, the man's elderly mother, who spoke almost no English at all, knocked on my front door and handed me a gorgeous flower from her yard. It was not a cutting ; the roots were healthy where she had gently dug it from the ground. The incident began a warm friendship for us which mostly consisted of waves and head nods from our respective yards.

So this was the stuff of my life, walking my beloved dogs every morning, rain or star shine, heading off to a job I loved, returning home to the sound of my grandchildren's laughter. As far as I was concerned, life could have gone on that way year after year. But as I have learned in the course of my journey, change is inevitable.

In a single year, my life changed more dramatically than I could have imagined. Besides starting a new job in the fall of 2002, I had also begun working on a new book. During the long summer months prior, I had gone back through a thick file filled with information about my great-grandmother, Bertha Gifford. She had been accused in 1928 of murdering a number of people by poisoning them with arsenic. This had been a family secret my mother had not shared with me until my sister inadvertently revealed it in a casual conversation one day. Since that time, and when I finally had my mother's permission to do so, I'd been gathering information about Bertha's life. Finally in that summer, surrounded by newspaper clippings and pages of notes, I had felt compelled to tell her story. So in that fall of 2002 when I began teaching at Upland High, I also began writing my second book.

Work on the manuscript progressed slowly during the school year as might be imagined. On weekdays I found it nearly impossible to get any writing done; I was simply too tired by the end of the day to be creative. But on weekends, after the dogs were walked, I would often shut myself in my bedroom to squint over newspaper accounts of her alleged crimes and try to create my own images with words that would convey the truth, not the sensationalized drivel meant to sell papers.

By the following June, I was eager for my time off in summer so that I could spend long hours writing. In addition, I wanted to take a trip to Missouri to fill in some holes in my research.

And while I was immersed in studying the psyches of serial killers, Shali had begun spending time with a man who was a far cry from the broken and abusive Dustin. Joseph was an army veteran, had a stable job with a school district, was divorced with a little girl who was two years younger than Hali. The five of them—Shali, Joseph, Ben, Hali and Reese—were pretty much an instant family.

Because of this, Shali spent less time at home and more time with the man who would eventually become her second husband. I missed my grandkids when they weren't around on the weekends, but the sudden silence of the house gave me creative space in which to write, and when the school year ended in June, I set a goal of finishing the book on Bertha before I went back to work at the end of August.

As I plunged further into the research and writing, Shali and Joseph began their life together by moving into an apartment. Now it was me, the three dogs and the two cats. I was forty-nine years old. It was the first time in my life I lived alone.

And so I wrote every day, sometimes four or five hours at a stretch. I walked the dogs early, as always, and then, in between small home improvement projects, I wrote. I finished the manuscript the Sunday before the new school year started, and it was a good thing I did; there were more life changes in store for me.

Within weeks after Shali moved out, Ian began to deteriorate. I honestly believe that, without his tiny herd of children to watch over, he lost his will to live. He quickly became lethargic on our walks, meandering listlessly instead of dragging me along. When he began vomiting repeatedly one day, I took him to the vet. The ever-jovial Dr. Olmstead had retired and sold her practice to a male vet I didn't care for, but he had a young assistant, Dr. Han, who was gentle with the animals and also good with people. He examined Ian, found nothing out of the ordinary, and suggested the dog might have eaten something that disagreed with him. He seemed fine for a week, then the vomiting began again. This time when we saw Dr. Han, I had another issue to discuss as well: Ian had become aggressive, almost vicious. One morning when he'd crept into my bedroom to try to get to the cats' food, I saw him and waved him away, as I'd done a thousand times before. Instead of turning tail and scurrying out, he stood his ground, bared his teeth and snarled at me. I hoped his behavior that day was an aberration. It wasn't. He'd become more aggressive with every passing day.

Because of my daily routine of walking the dogs first thing in the morning, it had been relatively easy to collect a urine specimen from Ian. Based on those results, Dr. Han drew a blood sample. When the lab results came in, he called me. Ian's kidneys were shutting down. In his quiet voice he talked about extraordinary measures that might prolong Ian's life for awhile, but ultimately would not save it. Given his increasingly aggressive behavior coupled with his age—he was fourteen now—and other health factors, it seemed there was a decision to be made.

It took me a week. Every morning I would walk the dogs and watch Ian as he became more lethargic, more anxious and uncomfortable, and each time I would return to the house thinking, *one more day.* Finally, I knew it was unfair to him to withhold relief simply because doing the right thing would be painful for me. I made the appointment, took him in, and sat on the floor of the exam room holding him in my arms while Dr. Han helped him leave this world behind. Afterward, I took his body home and buried it near where we had buried Alex. I wanted Ian's children to be able to visit his grave, though I knew his spirit had moved on to the place where good dogs are rewarded for their unconditional love and guardianship.

The next day I took Ellie and Osa across the street to the park and let them run off leash while I slowly followed behind them, mourning the loss of our dour yet devoted companion.

And it seemed our fate that one curmudgeon would be replaced by another.

My mother, now eighty-four, was declining rapidly. After surgery to replace a knee, she'd begun using a walker and had never moved past her dependence on it. She'd caused a serious traffic accident by making a left turn in front of on-coming traffic, so she made the tough decision (with our persuasion) to stop driving, which meant one of us, either my brother, my sister or I, were required to take her to her frequent medical appointments. When I invited her to move in with me, I thought she would decline, given our life-long lack of a mother-daughter bond and the fact that she would have to move fifty miles south to the Inland Empire. But my mother's thinking could be counted on to be contrary to mine.

I'd finished my book and the school year had started in August. Ian died in September. And in October, my mother moved in with me.

Forty-eight hours later we had a major confrontation after I came home from work and called my son, talking to him for over an hour, catching up on his life. Mom resented being "ignored," and she demanded I put in a separate phone line for her.

Prior to my trip to Missouri and my work on the book about Mom's grandmother, I would have argued with her. But that trip, that work, had changed me, enabling me to see my mother through a journalist's eyes instead of a daughter's. It was much easier to forgive her now, as I understood more fully the tragic beginnings of her life.

The next morning I left her a note with the number for the phone company, instructing her to call if she wanted that separate line. She never did.

Three weeks after she moved in, the world around us was ablaze.

Southern California is notorious for wildfires in the fall. When the hot, dry Santa Ana winds charge in, they steal every drop of moisture from every living thing. That October, as the winds blew, someone started a fire in San Bernardino, and it just kept marching west, advancing along the foothills, burning everything in sight. For days the air was filled with smoke and soot and burning embers, so thick the neighborhood was a ghost town, everyone hunkering down inside. Several days in, the electricity went out on our block. Fortunately it was a weekend, so Mom and I read books and played Scrabble, lighting candles even in daytime as the heavy smoke blotted out the sun. Three days later power was restored. Small blessings such as hot water are more greatly appreciated when one is forced to live without them for a time.

For weeks after the fires were finally extinguished, I went out every Saturday, driving to the burned areas, taking pictures to document the devastation... because I couldn't believe my eyes. The San Bernardino mountains had burned savagely. The foothills from Interstate 15 west to Mt. Baldy had been reduced to piles of ash. Nothing lived. Miraculously, firefighters had stopped the towering flames from heading up San Antonio Canyon, and Mt. Baldy Village had been spared. Afterward, my students who lived in San Antonio Heights, at the foot of Baldy, would tell me stories about their cell phones going off during the annual homecoming dance, frantic parents summoning them home to help evacuate, a task they performed still clad in formal attire.

For me, the fires were a bookmark in time, symbolizing all that had changed in recent times. I had lost Ian, and I had lost the comfort and consolation my grandchildren provided when they lived under my roof. In exchange, I now lived with the constant criticism and tension Mom brought with her. In Ben and Hali's presence, I had enjoyed the undeserved but god-like status of being incapable of doing anything wrong. Now, in Mom's eyes, I was incapable of doing anything right, and the foul mood of my home hung on me like the sour smell that lingered for weeks after the fires.

When Shali moved out and Mom moved in, I had converted my third bedroom into an office with my big writing desk, my computer and my file cabinet. In that first year after Mom arrived, I spent a great deal of time in that room, searching for publishers who might be interested in the book about my great-grandmother.

I wrote query letters, sent out book proposals—all the work writers do when trying to move the finished product from manuscript form to published book. I was still freelancing, and I had some significant sales that year, to the Los Angeles Times, the Writer magazine, the Christian Science Monitor and others. But no one wanted to publish my personal narrative on discovering the truth about my great-grandmother's alleged crimes. I thought the story was compelling, but at that time, Bertha Gifford had been all but lost to local folklore, and as one agent told me, "No one's ever heard of *you*."

A year passed, and then another. I walked the lady dogs every morning, took care of my mother, wrote when I could, and tried to keep believing that I'd find a publisher for the book I titled *Tainted Legacy*. I rarely dated as I rarely met new people, and when I did, I never really connected with anyone.

My stress level increased as Mom's health issues multiplied. And she was not the only one whose health was deteriorating.

Ellie's incontinence had returned; the medication was no longer effective. Our morning walks now were strolls, as Ellie's arthritis kept her stiff and uncomfortable. At times I gave her baby aspirin to alleviate her discomfort, as just getting up from the floor was painful for her. She had lost her healthy roundness and now her skin hung on her like an old carcass.

I discussed her condition with my vet and with Dan. They both used the phrase "quality of life." With Ian, the decision to help him cross over was a tough one, but necessary considering his illness. Ellie's decline had been gradual, as if each day a bit more life drained from her, and it broke my heart to see it.

Finally, after watching her one day struggle for several long minutes to stand, then limp to the back door, tail wagging slowly as she asked to be let out, I knew it was time. I knew because our eyes met, and I understood that she trusted me to care for her in whatever way was best.

Once again I sat on the floor of the exam room holding a big dog in my arms and crying as Dr. Han gently released her from her pain.

I have two photos of Ellie that I love. In one, she is stretched out on her huge fluffy pancake of a dog bed, one of her plush toys clamped in her jaws, looking for all the world like some regal lioness. The other end of that toy is held by tiny Hali at three years of age as she engages in a lopsided tug-of-war with this gentle giant of a dog. The other picture is of Ellie lying on her back in the green grass of the backyard, her paws in the air. She is smiling, the end of her pink tongue protruding from her front teeth.

Ellie's response to the world—even when she was in pain—was one of unwavering joy and curiosity. I loved that about her, and her readiness, even in her old age, to play. I still miss her sunny disposition every day.

CHAPTER FIFTEEN

My mother and both brothers later told me that I had given Ellie a great life in her final years. Their words were little comfort as I silently and sadly considered that my one remaining dog was nearly sixteen.

Osa and I still walked every morning, but like Ellie, Osa's arthritis gradually made movement difficult and painful. We walked slowly, and we didn't go far. I found a dog bed that made lying down easier for her; she would simply line her body up with the rectangular pillow and crumple onto her side.

As the only-dog, I must confess that Osa was pretty spoiled. I doted on her because I missed Ellie and Ian, and also because I had bonded so closely with her. Mom enjoyed her company during the day while I was at work, and she kept to my side when I was at home, so between the two of us she received nearly constant attention and affection. When she first came to me, it had taken months before Osa would stand still and allow me to groom her. Now a daily brushing was part of our routine. Her coat was soft and beautiful, and when she stretched out next to me on the family room floor in the evenings, I would run the brush over and over through her long, silky hair.

Calpurnia actually became jealous of the attention lavished on a mere dog, so I bought a small cat brush and groomed her every night as well, a practice which greatly reduced the amount of cat hair on my bedspread.

Boo had a different response to Osa. While he had always been wary of the other two dogs, often retreating to his safe place in the closet when they were indoors, Osa's gentle spirit seemed to win him over. In the morning after our walk while I made her breakfast, Boo would emerge from the bedroom and sidle up beside her, leaning into her body and rubbing against her legs. I'm afraid his affection remained unrequited, but Osa would stand tolerantly as the big cat stroked her fur with his body, meowing and purring happily.

In the second year that Mom lived with me, she began to have Transit Ischemic Attacks or "ministrokes." The first time she fell and couldn't get up, she crawled around on the floor for over an hour before finding a way to boost herself up on some low furniture, relating the story of her mishap to me in anxious tones when I returned home from work that day.

The next time she fell it was just as I was drifting off to sleep one night. I heard a crash from her room accompanied by a sharp cry of pain; her arm had hit the corner of a night table as she fell. She was bleeding profusely from the wound when I got to her, and the pain rendered her arm useless so that she couldn't help herself get up. Placing her good arm around my neck, I lifted her up and onto her bed, then (under her glaring scrutiny) I dressed and bandaged her arm where a large patch of skin had torn away. She refused to let me take her to the emergency room, and it took weeks for the wound to heal.

One night, close to midnight, she fell out of bed—or said she did. As I ran to her room, I found her sitting in a corner, wild-eyed. In between moaning and nervously brushing her hair back from her face, she would look up at me with little recognition, and I knew she'd suffered another TIA. I called 9-1-1, and the paramedics who arrived were great with her, gently lifting her up and helping her, upon her insistence, to the bathroom like a quartet of gallant knights, then waited for her to emerge, standing in my narrow hallway and making small talk while my mother peed and dutifully washed her hands. When she opened the door, they escorted her back to her bed, all the while trying, in soft tones, to persuade her to let them take her to the hospital. They nearly charmed her into it. (When I asked her the next day if she remembered what had transpired the night before, she replied, "I know the paramedics were here. A couple of them were really good looking," which let me know she had returned to her usual feistiness.) But no. Mom and I'd had some prior experiences, once when she had felt like she couldn't catch her breath and another time with a previous TIA, in which we'd had her transported to the hospital "just to get checked out," and both times had resulted in exhausting ordeals for both of us. One of those times she ended up in the hospital for two days, and in lying prone all that time she developed blood clots in her legs, which led to yet another life-threatening incident.

I know that Mom's hope was that she would simply die at home, as she told me often that she didn't want to "die among strangers," a reference to going into assisted living. I had hoped that would be the case for her as well. But she simply continued to decline, and there came a point at which I just couldn't care for her at home any longer. Or if I did, I'd have to quit my job to be her caregiver full time. After talking it over with Kevin, who agreed with me completely, I sat down to have the talk with my mother that many of us from the "baby boomer" generation dread.

I had expected her to be resistant. But she never disagreed with me. She knew how much I worried about her while I was at work, afraid she would fall and hurt herself. I woke every time she did at night, unable to fall back to sleep until I knew she had safely navigated the perilous journey from bedroom to bathroom and back again. Mom understood that, for both our sakes, she needed to be in a place that provided more extensive safety features and around-the-clock care if she needed it. In the end, she thanked me for taking care of her, an acknowledgement which surprised and touched me deeply.

When she moved out, Kevin bought her a motorized chair, and in no time, the aid to mobility had her whizzing up and down the corridors of her assisted living residence. I couldn't feel too bad for her; within months she had two male suitors, both very nice gentlemen, one of whom eventually proposed to her, though she turned him down.

The house had become profoundly quiet. My children were all busy living the lives of young adults. While I was pleased for their independence, I missed them terribly at times, missed the days of loading all four plus Niki and Alex into the old station wagon for a trip to the park... missed the days after Shali's divorce when I would arrive home to the aroma of dinner and the sound of my grandchildren's voices calling out "Nana's home!" as they raced each other through the house to greet me.

I felt at odds with my life, as if I were marking time in "the waiting room of the world," as C. S. Lewis put it. My children were gone to pursue their dreams. I had written a book that no one wanted to publish. My mother had moved out of my care and into someone else's. I thought I should write, but the disappointment in not publishing *Tainted Legacy* weighed on me, opened up a portal through which my inner critic would daily convince me there was no use writing if no one would ever read my words. Where once my house had seemed too small with its kids, grandkids, cats and dogs, now it had become a hollow shell that echoed when I spoke to Osa, Boo or Cal.

And Osa never met me at the door anymore. Now in her sixteenth year, she slept most of the time, and her hearing had diminished to the point where she just didn't hear the truck pull into the garage or my key turn the lock in the door. I would find her on her dog bed, deep in sleep, and she would first startle when I gently shook her shoulder to wake her, then slowly wag her tail at the realization that I had, once more, returned home to her.

Mornings had similar but more complex issues. Osa slept so deeply at night, it had become progressively harder and harder to wake her. Each morning after I switched off the alarm, I leaned over the side of the bed, reaching down to pet her and talk to her. She would not stir from her sleep, and her body seemed so still at times, her breathing so shallow, I sometimes thought she had died in the night.

To get her up, I had to physically lift her, one hand held gently under her ribcage, the other holding and steadying her as I pulled her to her feet. She was frail and thin, capable now of walking only as far as the parkway at the end of the driveway. She would squat, do her business which I would promptly pick up, then we would slowly make our way back inside where she would eat, drink, then limp slowly back down the hall to her bed.

One morning as I led her down the driveway for our walk, she stopped in her tracks. I spoke to her quietly, tugging ever so gently on her leash. The stiffness in her joints was simply too painful for her to take another step. She stared at me with the same look Ellie had given me a year before. They were such good dogs. And they wanted to be with me every step of the way. But Osa had reached the time when her journey would lead her away from me. I knelt beside her on the cold concrete, my arms around her neck, tears falling onto her fur. Then I carefully picked her up and carried her to the grass, supporting her while she relieved herself.

And so I made one more appointment with Dr. Han, who quietly left the room afterward as I sobbed uncontrollably, Osa's still body wrapped in my arms.

Ian was really always Ben's dog. Ellie was really always Dan's dog. But Osa had entwined her heart with mine, and part of me was simply lost after she was gone. For weeks, the only time I wasn't crying was while I was at work. In the mornings, I awoke depressed, grief hanging over me in the darkness. I had no dogs to walk. I returned home in the afternoon to sleeping cats who purred for a few minutes as I stroked their fur, then curled their heads around and went back to sleep.

Calpurnia, seventeen, died several months after Osa did.

And so it was me and Boo, who spent his days sleeping and his nights slinking around like a panther in the neighbor's jungle of a backyard.

The house no longer seemed like a home to me; the echoing rooms held only memories now.

I needed a change, to sink down new roots some-where, start a new adventure, find my way out of the dark forest of sadness before I became a victim of despair.

Driving home from Mt. Baldy after a mid-winter hike one day, I rolled past cabins with wood smoke drifting from chimneys into the clean, cold air. I wondered what it would be like to live there. At home, I called Catherine, a friend and colleague at Upland High who lived in Mt. Baldy.

"Catherine," I said, after we'd exchanged pleasantries, "tell me all the good things and all the bad things about living in Mt. Baldy."

"Kay," she replied, "there are no bad things."

A few months later, I bought a cabin in the forest. I put my house on the market and began packing and preparing for what would prove to be one of the greatest adventures of my life.

Ellie, Ian and Osa were all twelve when they came to be with me. Fifty years ago, twelve was old for a dog. Nowadays, with better choices in nutritional dog food and our knowledge of a dog's need for daily exercise (as well as our own), dogs can easily enjoy life well into their teens. These three made terrific companions as senior dogs, and as heartbreaking as it was to lose them, I am ever grateful for their presence during that handful of years. They gave my life a sense of structure and routine, taught me the joy of getting outside first thing every morning, rain or shine, which gifted me with over a thousand blessed and meditative dawns.

Had Ian gone to a shelter, I am convinced he would've had little chance of being adopted, and his life would have quickly come to a sad end. Instead, he spent his last years as young Ben's devoted guardian, and on one particular morning kept me from being robbed... or perhaps a much worse fate.

Ellie's exuberant joy was infectious in my family, and having her always near was like having a living, breathing fuzzy teddy bear to hug.

And my beloved Osa was just the right dog to take over Alex's job of welcoming me home, muzzle first, at the door every night.

I could not be with Rufus, Sapo and Alex in their twilight years. I believe that Ellie, Ian and Osa were brought to me as a recompense. They filled those years of my life with sweet companionship. In return, I lavished them with all the reminiscent affection I carried for the first three dogs of my life. I am diminished by their loss, while at the same time I am enriched, my life enhanced one thousand fold by the time they walked with me.

As I write these words, it is winter, 2012. The mountain is shrouded in clouds today, and it is no less beautiful than when the sun pours through the canopy of leaves from the tall trees that surround me here. A light snow is falling. I am resisting the urge to throw on my boots and jacket and walk out into the quiet forest to watch the snowflakes drift down into the canyon below my cabin. There is much to do as I am preparing, after five years on the mountain, to move back down to the valley below. The adventures I've had here—with bears and bobcats, deer and bighorn sheep, fire, flood and feasting—are tales for another book. First and foremost, before I go, I need to finish the story of my good dogs. I need to write that story here, in the serenity of the mountain, because my heart has broken in reliving these stories again. Thank goodness this place is a place of healing.

I assumed Osa would be my last dog for a long, long time, as I knew that moving to the mountain would limit my ability to keep a dog. In a sense, she was. But I would be remiss if I did not mention two dogs who will always hold a special place in my heart, two dogs sent to comfort me by Heaven, Fate, the

Universe—whatever you are willing to believe. I can only say I know that they were sent... because their timing was perfect.

In the months while I waited for my house to sell, I received an email from an acquaintance who was a volunteer at an animal shelter in San Bernardino County, a shelter notorious for being a high-kill facility. (Administrators there euthanized over 11,000 animals in 2010 alone.) Becky—not her real name—would work with dogs there who were slated to be put down, walking them, taking their pictures, then posting desperate ads on craigslist, trying to find adoptive homes for them before their time was up. Becky's email to me described a small black dog that had been an owner drop off. The dog had been virtually ignored by staff and potential adopters since its arrival as it stayed mostly at the back of its kennel. She had taken it out one day and discovered a sweet affectionate girl who was well behaved, walked well on a leash, and loved belly rubs. Becky knew that I was mourning the death of Osa.

"I know your heart is hurting," she said. "But you should just come and look at her."

I did. But try as I might, I could not get her to even approach the front of the large outdoor kennel where she was housed with two other dogs. She didn't act frightened. She seemed aloof, lying quietly and staring off into the distance while the other two dogs wiggled at the front of the cage, begging me to get them out. I returned home to email Becky that I could not make a connection with the poor thing.

But of course, I couldn't stop thinking about her. And later that night, from out of the blue, a thought materialized in my brain. I went back the next day and asked a shelter worker to bring her out so I could walk her. In doing so I confirmed that lightning bolt of a thought: This little dog was deaf. Once outside the kennel, she looked at me, eyes locked on mine, to determine what I wanted of her. I stepped forward with the leash, and she was immediately at my side, walking nicely. Away from the noise of the other dogs, I tried speaking to her, snapping my fingers, making clucking sounds. She only responded to the leash.

She smelled terribly and her long curly hair was matted and filthy. I took her home that day.

Ben came for a visit a few days later and he helped me clean her up, sitting with me for hours as we first clipped all of her matted fur away, then washed her. She never resisted, complying easily with everything we asked of her, as long as she understood what we wanted.

"She's amazing," I told Ben, "some kind of mystical being. But she needs a name."

"Why don't you call her Mystic?" he replied.

Perfect.

I had brought her home at the end of summer, and so in those leisurely days before I had to go back to work, I took her everywhere—to the dog park where she played joyously with other dogs, up to Mt. Baldy to see the waterfall and splash in the creek, and along the trail in the foothills that was Alex's favorite. At night she would settle in quietly on the blanket I put down for her, responding quickly to my hand signal to lie down.

A free vet check was part of the adoption agreement, so I took her in to see my vet about a week after bringing her home. Dr. Han wasn't working that day, and the senior vet did the examination. Halfway through it he stopped to ask me where I'd gotten her. When I told him, he asked why I'd adopted her and whether I intended to keep her.

"Of course," I told him. "That's why I'm here."

He made a grunting sound and began to list off all her issues; she was old, she was deaf, she was losing her sight to cataracts. Worst of all, he showed me the inside of her mouth, expressing great disdain as he did so. Her gums had grown up over her teeth, indicating extreme old age—and profound neglect.

"Can it be treated?" I asked. It could, but the surgery would be expensive.

While the doctor shook his head at my folly, I hugged Mystic to my chest. She deserved as many good days as I could give her. I made an appointment with the receptionist, and two days later we were back. When the vet tech came out to the waiting room to take her in, I kissed Mystic on the nose, then motioned with my hand for her to "go," and she immediately complied. It was the last time I ever saw her. She didn't survive the surgery.

As I walked in the forest in the hours after I received the call from the vet's receptionist, I wondered how this amazing little dog had ended up at the shelter. And just as the truth of her deafness had come to me, so her story played out in my head, and I have to believe it is what truly happened, that she was once a beloved family pet. But time passed. No longer the cute puppy, she was ignored and neglected. In order to save themselves the guilt of having her put to sleep, the family simply dropped her off at the shelter, knowing she had little chance of being adopted and that in a matter of days, the shelter personnel would do the dirty work of ending her life.

She was with me for less than two weeks. But in that time, she had the chance to be the beloved puppy again, to be loved and spoiled and given the attention and affection she deserved. And she taught me that no matter how badly our hearts our breaking, we are still capable of reaching out, of loving deeply, of making room in our hearts even while we are grieving the loss of another.

In March of 2010, my mother passed away at the age of ninety-one. A year and a half earlier, I was finally able to place in her hands a published copy of *Tainted Legacy*, the book about her grandmother. Our relationship changed because of it. For nearly eighty years, my mother had lived with the well-guarded family secret and unsolved mystery of a grandmother who had loved her and raised her but had been vilified by her community. The book gave my mother closure, allowed her to let go of the shame she had carried for most of her life. She was grateful to me for doing the research, for writing the book, for never giving up on seeing it in print, and ultimately, for understanding her life-long pain over the events of those days long ago.

For a brief time before she passed, Mom was on hospice care in my brother's home. Returning from what proved to be our last visit with her, my son and I noticed a frightened dog cowering in the weeds by a freeway offramp in Rancho Cucamonga. Overwrought with emotion, I made Ezra pull over so I could try to coax the dog out of hiding, but he resisted our attempts to get close to him, and eventually a California Highway Patrol officer arrived, telling us other drivers had called 9-1-1 and animal control would be responding. This incident occurred in the months following the collapse of the U.S. economy, when shelters were filled to over capacity with owner relinquished dogs. I wondered if his family had simply dropped him off out here, hoping that someone else would rescue him and give him a home. In those days, it happened a lot.

Several days later I visited the Rancho shelter just to see if they had been able to catch the dog and bring it in. Once again I found myself following that inner voice that simply compelled me to go there. While walking through the rows of kennels, I was halted in my tracks by the soft brown eyes of a beautiful dog who looked more plush toy than canine. She was a Sheltie and Corgi mix, her coat a mix of white, tan and brown. She had a long Sheltie muzzle—like Sapo and Osa—and shorter, Corgi legs. It was love at first sight for me. Her face was bright and attentive, and she stood inside the chain link looking up at me expectantly. I knelt down next to her.

"Sit," I said.

She sat immediately, continuing to stare with her searching eyes. I knew what she wondered. She wanted to know if I would be the one to rescue her.

But I just couldn't. I had no yard, nowhere to put her during the day while I was at work. Leaving her inside alone for all those hours was out of the question. The year before I had lost Boo to cancer and now lived with one small black cat—Sugar Plum—who was terrified of dogs.

Yet here was another dog whose heartstrings simply wound around mine.

I asked at the front desk if I could take her out and walk her, just to get her out of the cage. I took her out in the early spring sunshine, and we spent a half hour first walking, then just sitting comfortably in the grass together. I stroked her soft ears, and she licked my hand repeatedly. When I finally, reluctantly, took her back inside, the animal control officer told me her story. A man had come to drop her off. He seemed agitated, she said. When he was asked to provide proof that he lived in Rancho Cucamonga, he refused, became belligerent and stormed out into the parking lot where he tied the small dog to a utility pole, got in his truck and drove away, abandoning her there. She was so frightened that when officers went out to bring her in, she jerked out of her collar and ran off. Luckily, she didn't run far, just hid in the bushes surrounding the parking lot. It took them days of taking food out to her before officers finally won her trust and brought her inside to safety.

For three days I stayed away from the Rancho shelter, thinking of her constantly but hoping some very fortunate family had adopted her. I returned on a Thursday. She was still there. Now she was beginning to show signs of extreme stress and anxiety. Her eyes were glassy with fear, and she trembled constantly.

I went back up to the front and filled out adoption papers. When I walked her out to my truck, I opened the door, and she jumped right in, sitting primly in the backseat, her gaze turned to look out the window as if she'd done this a thousand times before.

Almost immediately I began calling her Harper, after Harper Lee, author of *To Kill a Mockingbird*.

As I had no dog food, I had to stop at Petsmart on the way home. I took her in with me, and the experience reminded me of when my children were pretty little babies; people kept coming up to fawn over her and tell me how beautiful she was. It took me nearly an hour to pick up the few things I needed to care for her.

That night, I made her as comfortable as I could in the kitchen on a pile of blankets, told her to stay, and closed the door. I never heard a sound out of her all night. The next morning, bright and early, she met me at the kitchen door with tail wags and hand licks. Out the door we went, and for the first time in years, I had a dog to walk before dawn.

As it was Friday, and I had to go to work, I scooped up her blanket and some food, and back down the mountain we went. She spent most of the day curled up on her blanket in my classroom (unbeknownst to my principal) underneath my desk. Each time a new class period began, I called her out and had her meet my students. For the first five minutes every hour, she was a rock star, with kids crowded around her on the floor, each one begging to take her home. Cell phones emerged from backpacks (with my permission), photos were taken, pleading calls made home to moms and dads. By the end of the day, though, no one had gotten permission to take her, and so we simply headed back up the mountain.

That day was the last Friday before my spring break, so I had some time before I had to return to work. I took a photo of Harper the next day, posted an ad on craigslist, and then took her out for a hike up to the waterfall.

Really, and I'm not exaggerating, she was the perfect dog, just like Mystic. She walked well on the leash, came to me when I called her (after only having been with me for forty-eight hours), loved kids and other dogs. While at the waterfall, we encountered some hikers with two pit bulls and a German Shepherd. I asked if we could walk along with them, and Harper joined right in, wagging her tail and splashing with the other dogs in the stream.

By Saturday evening, I'd received five replies to the craigslist ad, five potential families pleading with me to let them adopt her. I began calling them on Sunday morning, and finally had it narrowed down to two. I visited both, and late on Sunday afternoon, made the decision to leave her with a family in Rancho Cucamonga. The young mom and dad had been looking for a puppy for their four-year-old daughter, but when they saw Harper's picture and read her story, they desperately wanted her. We walked around their upscale apartment complex, the little girl holding Harper's leash and intermittently stopping to throw her arms around the dog's neck. It seemed like the perfect fit.

Twenty-four hours later I returned from a long hike to a voicemail from the father: He had taken his daughter to a doctor's appointment, leaving Harper alone in the apartment with a window open. She had pushed out the screen and run off. They had looked everywhere for her around the complex. She was nowhere to be found. I put my head in my hands and sobbed. This little dog had gone through so much, and now she was homeless again, running the streets in unfamiliar territory. And it was pouring rain.

Days went by. I was an emotional wreck. I had lost my mom, but Harper had come into my life, giving me a reason to smile during the days when I was first grieving. The idea that she was somewhere out in the world, unsafe, plunged me back into sorrow that knew no words.

Then I returned home from another long hike in the forest to find a voicemail from a young girl who said, "My name is McKenna. I think I have your dog...."

The Rancho shelter had micro-chipped Harper before they released her to me. When McKenna and her father saw the little dog running in the street, they followed her until they had her cornered, then she simply surrendered herself to them. As responsible citizens, they took her to their vet who scanned her for a chip... which is what put them in touch with me.

It took me several minutes to get my emotions in check before I could call McKenna. She lived in Rancho, just a few miles from the family who had adopted Harper. I told her I would be there within the hour. Before I left, I called the young man who had naively left a window open with a new dog in the house. I thought he would be pleased that she'd been found. Instead, he told me they didn't want her back, that their landlord had been angry about the damaged screen. Just as well, I thought, and took off down the mountain to retrieve my little girl.

When I pulled up to McKenna's house, she walked outside, carrying Harper in her arms like a baby. I introduced myself, and I talked with McKenna and her father for a long time, telling them Harper's story, which only made McKenna love her all the more. Eventually, her father agreed that Harper could stay with them—on a trial basis, to see if she would fit in with the family. They had a very sweet, very old golden retriever who had already come to enjoy Harper's company, and their property was large with plenty of dog room to run. Again, it seemed like the perfect fit, and I drove away thrilled at this turn of events. But again, it didn't work out.

One day shy of Harper's trial period, McKenna's father called to say they wouldn't be able to keep her. McKenna was involved in her school's 4H club, and as a project she kept baby bunnies and chicks. Harper was fixated on them, and the family feared leaving her alone with them as her interest seemed predatory. I understood. Harper was very well-behaved at my house, but as soon as she spied my cat, all her herding ancestry emerged, and she just wanted to give chase. Poor Sugar Plum spent some anxious days while we fostered Harper.

McKenna's family offered to keep Harper until I could find a suitable home for her. I re-posted the ad to craigslist and waited. Again, in a matter of hours, there were several people interested in adopting her. I worked my way through the emails, eventually doing phone interviews with several of the respondents. One of those people was the mother of five boys. Her sons had grown up with small animals, and the family was ready for their first dog. They were excited at the prospect of welcoming Harper into their fold. They picked her up from McKenna's the following afternoon. Twenty-four hours later I received an urgent message on my cell phone. I called the mother to learn that she had spent most of the previous night in a hospital emergency room with her youngest son. Turns out he was acutely allergic to dogs.

Harper was returned to McKenna, and we started over yet another time.

One particular gentle voiced woman I spoke with lived alone in a condominium. I had hoped to find Harper a home with children because she seemed to come alive when kids were present, but Patti's kindness and empathy were so apparent in our phone conversation, I decided that, after all Harper had been through, connecting the two might be perfect for both of them. Patti picked up Harper from McKenna, then called me later to tell me how quickly she had fallen in love with this amazing little dog. For the first few days, she took her everywhere with her, just as I had done. But then Patti had to go back to work, leaving Harper alone all day. She came home to find major damage to her woodwork and doors where the frantic dog had tried to claw her way out of the house. To her credit, Patti went above and beyond to try to work out Harper's separation anxiety, but in the end, we all had to agree that the placement just wasn't going to work.

Again I re-posted the craigslist ad, this time editing the ad to include her need for someone who could stay with her during the day, at least until she worked through this new issue. And that's when I met Shannon Cloud through an email she sent. Or should I say, whoever those angels were who were looking out for Harper in the first place connected us. Which is how one little dog who was abandoned in Rancho Cucamonga ended up living the high life just this side of heaven in Ladera Ranch, California.

A month after Shannon took her home, she sent the following email to me and to Patti, who had continued to care for Harper while we found her final forever home:

Hey guys,

Just wanted to update you on Harper. She is still doing awesome and we love her so much! Everywhere that we go we get compliments on her great disposition. I've taken her to the local dog parks and she loves it. We tackled the separation issue, I think. We started out by taking her everywhere and leaving her in the car for 10-20 minutes. We started the same at home and so far we have gotten up to 2 hours with no property damage! She is such a sweetheart and LOVES the children. We had a dental assessment done. Poor girl has a broken tooth (which Patti told me about when we got her), an abscess and a ton of tartar. We are taking her in next week to get her all fixed up. I really think she was meant for us. Thank you to you both!

And then, a year and a half later, just as I was finishing the last section of this book, I received the following email from Shannon:

Hello Kay! We just wanted to write you to let you know how grateful we are that you saved Harper from that shelter! She is the sweetest dog that I have ever known. She is doing wonderful with us and is definitely a part of the family! Harper has decided pretty much from the beginning that she is MY dog, lol! She is always by my side. I take her just about everywhere that I can and boy does that make her happy! She is in excellent physical condition and gets regular exercise. (She loves making new doggie friends.) Just wanted to let you know that I think of you often and am forever in debt to you for this wonderful gift that you have given to us.

Hope that you are well,
Shannon

Sometimes it takes a community of dog lovers to rescue a single dog. But when we are motivated by love, miracles can happen.

My experience with Harper has made me realize that, while I am reluctant to leave this magical place of beauty, tranquility and healing, I can do so with excited anticipation. I have already begun working with a shelter and a rescue group, and once I am down the mountain, I will be able to foster more deserving dogs like Harper, providing the transition they need from rescue to life-long families.

And eventually, if I am lucky, perhaps the Universe will bring me at least one more good dog.

GRATITUDE

Thank you, Libby, Jennifer and Judy, my first readers, for your gently rendered comments and suggestions. Libby, I can't tell you how much I appreciate your close reading; thank you for saving me from throwing out my babies with the bath water!

Michael Welker, you have been my cheerleader from my first conceptualization of this project until the last page was written. Thank you for your friendship in my life; it has meant more than I can say.

Martin Lastrapes, thank you for being a cheerleader as well, and for sharing with me all your publishing savvy. It made all the difference. Thank you for always bringing the warmth and beauty of Chanel along with you, and you're right; we need to sit outside on patios more often. The world would certainly be a more serene place if everyone followed your advice.

Michael, Martin, Donna, Ezra and Mrs. Nick—thank you for your feedback on that one paragraph and mostly just for loving me.

Donna Staub, you didn't know it, but you were my audience as I wrote this book, my mentor in life, both in teaching and working with dogs. Your quiet light shines as a beacon in the Universe.

My thanks to Maureen Adams, author of *Shaggy Muses,* for so graciously allowing me to use the quote from her book, and for giving me something beautiful and literary to read while I worked on this book.

My humblest gratitude goes to every person I've ever met on the trail in Mt. Baldy who graciously complied when I asked, "Can I meet your dog?" Thank you so much for being willing to share the love and affection of your companion. It has meant the world to me in times when I was nearly too sad to speak.

Special thanks to TJ Murray, Lucky, Cookie Kueckels and the Black Dog for reminding me every day why it was so important to finish this book.

And to every volunteer in every animal rescue group across the country, including and especially the folks at H.O.P.E. rescue in Upland, California: Thank you for your time, your support, your sacrifice and the love you extend on behalf of those who cannot speak for themselves. You are all heroes in my book.